"One of the reasons why so many have so quickly taken to praying the Litany of Trust is because we need help to trust in God in the midst of various personal, ecclesial, and social struggles. In this life-changing work, we receive the grace to enter into the faith and contemplation of Sr. Faustina Bianchi, S.V., who prayed forth the Litany. She shows us how, with God's help, we can be delivered from the fears and false ideas that undermine trust and how to grow in the truths that will help us trust in God in every circumstance."

FR. ROGER J. LANDRY
Author of *Plan of Life: Habits to Help You Grow Closer to God*

"Trust is a highly valued virtue for Christians that few of us know how to achieve. In this book, you will learn not only how and why to trust the Lord but also that he is so very worthy of our trust. Sr. Faustina's gentle words are full of truth and the confidence that can come only from lived experience. In this powerful personal retreat, you, too, will discover the heart of the Father and the deep intimacy he desires to share with you as you surrender to his love."

BETH DAVIS
Writer, Director of Ministry Advancement for *Blessed is She*

"Life can overwhelm each and every one of us. There is only one solution: Jesus Christ! And in Sr. Faustina's retreat through the Litany of Trust, you will be welcomed into the depths of Jesus's unfailing love and mercy. I recommend this journey to all!"

CURTIS A. MARTIN
Founder and CEO of Fellowship of
Catholic University Students (FOCUS)

"The Litany of Trust is a gift for the world from God. And so is this book. I know I've been longing for something like *Jesus I Trust in You* since the first time I prayed the Litany of Trust, and I will be gifting this book to people for years to come!"

KATHRYN JEAN LOPEZ
Senior Fellow at National Review Institute and Director of the Center for Religion, Culture, and Civil Society

"Sr. Faustina's Litany of Trust now has a beautiful commentary to deepen our love for this indispensable virtue. Spiritual insights of simplicity and depth abound in this book, which each day focuses on a single verse in the Litany and amplifies it. Trust in God is especially needed today. To accept gracefully all that Our Lord gives us and all he takes from us is a measure of our love for him. Let us allow Sr. Faustina to lead us to a greater childlike confidence in God's providential care."

FR. DONALD HAGGERTY
Author of *Contemplative Enigmas: Insights and Aid on the Path to Deeper Prayer*

"Whether we find ourselves affected by circumstances beyond our control or a more personal challenge is staring us in the face, walking with Jesus through this beautiful Litany of Trust will help us move forward away from fear, bringing us one step closer to understanding and fulfilling the Lord's will for our lives."

TERESA TOMEO
Syndicated talk show host of *Catholic Connection*

JESUS

I TRUST
IN YOU

THE **ORIGINAL IMAGE** OF
DIVINE MERCY

ARCH. DIOCESIS VILNENSIS
VILNIAUS
ARKIVYSKUPIJA

WWW.ORIGINALDIVINEMERCY.COM

Sr. Faustina Maria Pia, S.V.

JESUS

I TRUST IN YOU

A 30-DAY PERSONAL RETREAT
with the
Litany of Trust

EMMAUS
ROAD
PUBLISHING
Steubenville, Ohio
www.emmausroad.org

Emmaus Road Publishing
1468 Parkview Circle
Steubenville, Ohio 43952

Library of Congress Control Number 2021939305
ISBN: 978-1-64585-144-8 (pb) / 978-1-64585-145-5 (eb)

Layout by Emily Demary
Cover design by Emily Demary and Patty Borgman

Nihil Obstat: Rev. James M. Dunfee, Censor Librorum
October 19, 2021
Imprimatur: Jeffrey M. Monforton, Bishop of Steubenville
October 19, 2021

The nihil obstat and imprimatur are declarations that a work is considered to be free from doctrinal or moral error. It is not implied that those who have granted the same agree with the content, opinions, or statements expressed.

Table of Contents

For all those who have had their hearts pierced.

"Those whose hearts are enlarged by confidence in God run swiftly on the path of perfection. . . . they are no longer weak as they once were. They become strong with the strength of God, which is given to all who put their trust in Him."

—St. Alphonsus Liguori—

Preface

I heard—not with my ears but in the silence of my heart—three words: "Litany of Trust." Taking out my journal without much thought, dozens of petitions flowed out from my heart.

It would seem that a prayer like the Litany of Trust would come from someone who perfectly trusted in the Lord. But the truth is, it was given to me because I needed trust. And somehow I sensed that others needed it too.

At that time, I was asking the Lord to help me find a way through an unexpected situation that left me feeling confused and alone. My heart was torn, as I was receiving conflicting advice from those I went to for guidance. Every time I thought about how to move forward, I felt tortured knowing that so much was at stake.

In my frustration I was praying for clarity. But for months, whenever I opened up the Scriptures, it was as though the Gospels only had one message: *Trust.* It did not matter whether Jesus was healing someone, welcoming sinners, or suffering unjustly—in every situation I felt Jesus' desire for me to recognize His unfailing goodness and deem Him trustworthy.

Looking at the crucifix in my room one Friday afternoon, a new courage came over me to finally stand in the truth of my profound need for God. Instead of feeling like a failure in His eyes, I was met with the realization that God wanted far more than to provide for my necessities. In these moments immediately prior to the inspiration to write the Litany of Trust, I had an experience which is impossible to capture in words. It was as though Jesus were gently lifting my chin to look at Him. It was as if He were saying, *"I don't want you to give your 'yes' to a set of circumstances, but to Me."*

Rather than consenting to any *plan*—my plan or the plan proposed by others—I was consenting to *Him*. Without having any other reason than knowing He was asking it, I was giving the gift of my love to Him. I was placing my trust in *Him* and not my own understanding. Instead of being held back by my complicated analysis, I could let Jesus have His way in me.

This relationship of love is what I wanted, even more than clarity or control. My heart was filled, or set free, with the desire to trust God with my life. As you'll discover in these pages, in the invitation of trust, we find not only ourselves but also a God who deeply desires our love.

Introduction

In our day and age, trust and mercy are as popular as tape recorders and fax machines: people wonder if they're still around and working. Yes, they are. And when combined, their credibility is off the charts.

Every day we trust a myriad of people and things. We trust bridges to hold us and restaurants to serve food we can safely consume. We trust that our hair will fall in almost the same way as it did yesterday and that our dog will be waiting for us to go out for a walk in the morning. We trust professors to teach valid material and doctors to prescribe what is best for our health.

Trust sounds straightforward, but in practice, trust can feel complicated if we've been mistaken about who or what to rely on. Unfulfilled promises, the abuse of authority, and encountering our own limitations, as well as betrayals on personal and corporate levels, can all fuel a strong distrust. Can trust once broken be restored? In a culture ravaged by dishonesty and relativism, is it even desirable to trust?

We can't avoid trust. When we fall short or others fail us, we scramble to find if there is anything unchanging to rely on. All of us are searching to trust something bigger than ourselves.

A Polish sister in the 1930s, Faustina Kowalska (whom I was named after at birth), filled many notebooks detailing the Lord's message to her, which asked the world to trust in His mercy. What, then, is this mercy of God, that it should be trusted?

When we think of mercy, we may cringe a little. We may not want to receive mercy because we do not want to be the one in need of mercy. And we may not want to give mercy because we do not desire or have the strength to love another who has wronged us. Mercy can be hard to receive and hard to give.

The mercy of God, however, goes beyond showing compassion for an offender. Although it is highlighted when meeting our sinfulness, God's mercy encompasses the fullness of His love for us, which is infinite and freely given, without conditions for earning it.

As creatures we are enveloped in God's mercy at every moment. The very creation of our life is undeserved. We did nothing to labor for it, nor can we return the favor. Without His unconditional, merciful love, we would simply not exist. Mercy is God's love for us, which is *always* unmerited. And there is no shortage of it!

In taking on our human nature, Jesus perfectly joined God and man in His very person. He embodies the encounter of God's love for humanity. In speaking to St. Faustina, Jesus expressed, "I am Love and Mercy Itself. There is no misery that could be a match for My mercy, neither will misery exhaust it, because as it is being granted—it increases. The soul that trusts in My mercy is most fortunate, because I Myself take care of it."[1]

Jesus would repeat many times the importance of trust, but this may be the clearest: "The graces of My mercy are drawn by means of one vessel only, and

---

[1] St. Maria Faustina Kowalska, *Diary of Saint Maria Faustina Kowalska: Divine Mercy in My Soul* (Stockbridge, MA: Marian Press, 1987), para. 1273.

that is—trust. The more a soul trusts, the more it will receive."[2] Trust is choosing to *receive* this unconditional love of God for us, His mercy.

What is more reliable than the mercy of God? It is total and inexhaustible, and everything for us.

THE HEART OF THE MATTER

In creating us, the Father imbued us with all our uniqueness, as a singular radiance of His life. We *are* because He willed us; He wanted us to be. His intentionality was not just a passing thought at our conception; we are *continually receiving* our being from the overflowing love of the Trinity.

As the psalmist says, "For you formed my inward parts, you knitted me together in my mother's womb. I praise you, for I am wondrously made" (Ps 139:13–14). *Each* of us is deeply known and chosen by God. We experience the truth of this within our hearts—our hearts being, as defined by the *Catechism of the Catholic Church*, "the dwelling-place where I am, where I live. . . . The heart is our hidden center." The *Catechism* continues by saying the heart is the place of decision and encounter (CCC 2563).

I like to picture the heart with two openings. On one side, we have an opening to receive our life and love continually from God, as well as to receive His love through others. On the other side, we each have another opening, for our life and love to be given away. The space in between is like a reservoir. This *open quality*

---

[2] Kowalska, *Diary of St. Faustina*, para. 1578.

of receiving and giving reveals to us that we have been made for relationship. It's written into us.

At the core of our person is the thirst to be loved and the unrelenting call to love. Yet in being open to love, we must be vulnerable. To be vulnerable is to risk the possibility of being hurt, harmed, or wounded physically or emotionally. We think of it often as opening ourselves in a way that may lead to pain or rejection—but I think of vulnerability as much more. It is a place of openness where we are invited into authentic relationship. C. S. Lewis said, "To love at all is to be vulnerable."[3]

In this broken world where love is not always reciprocated, we often experience this open quality of our hearts, this vulnerability, as insecurity, defenselessness, or lack of control. Because of the suffering we have encountered, it would be more comfortable to close the doors on these openings of our hearts. Rather than looking outside of ourselves to receive the love that reveals to us who we are, we find it safer to define ourselves. Or instead of taking the risk of sharing our love, we strive for an independence that does not need others, intent on achieving happiness on our own terms. Love is a choice; therefore, I have the freedom to keep the doors open or close them.

As soon as we start shutting the door to receiving love, the door on the other side of our heart slides shut as well. Giving and receiving move together. In fear, we end up stifling the very thing we most desire: love.

Trust is what opens the doors of our hearts to the flow of love. And through trusting God's merciful love, we open ourselves to the ever-flowing stream of God's

---

[3] C. S. Lewis, *The Four Loves* (New York: Harcourt Brace, 1991), 121.

victorious goodness. If we have been made to love, we have been made to be vulnerable and, therefore, created to live trust.

THE REVIVAL OF TRUST

Most of us are not aware of the thresholds of our trust and what makes us choose to shut the doors of our hearts. Usually it is not until a crisis hits us that we realize our need for greater openness, to trust someone greater than ourselves.

Jesus longs for the chance to show us how trust in Him conquers the storms of life and manifests the brilliance of His love. It is only through Jesus that we can learn to live authentic trust. In fully embracing our humanity, Jesus transforms the negative experience of our openness (this vulnerability), showing us it is *the* place of love, true life, and joy.

No matter what we face, He who is almighty invites us to meet Him in a life beyond our capacities—His divine life. Only His mercy can fix the shattered trust in our hearts.

God is always inviting us to a deeper relationship with Him and, therefore, a greater threshold of trust. In the pages ahead, I invite you to follow each invocation of the Litany of Trust to encounter ways of growing in trust. You'll find

- The experience of the human heart in the struggle to trust;
- Jesus' perspective that He longs for us to see; and

- The invitation to openness, to receive God in this powerful place of trust.

The Litany of Trust encompasses more than can possibly be captured in a few pages. I've focused on certain elements of each invocation, but the Lord will speak to your heart individually and uniquely. As you read each chapter, take time for prayer and reflection before continuing on, that it may truly be a retreat experience. A fitting close to your times of prayer is the Litany of Trust, included on page 195. I'll be united with you in prayer.

Jesus is always worth trusting.

DAY 1

From the belief that I have to earn Your love, deliver me, Jesus.

The world makes us think, whether through interactions with parents, teachers, coaches, or bosses, that with a little hard work, we can get what we want in life.

If I make straight As, I'm awarded a scholarship. If I push myself at practice, I'll have more playing time. If I put in longer hours at work, I'll get the promotion.

In the context of a reward system, it can even seem like love is bestowed on those who prove themselves to be deserving of it.

Solanus Casey was someone who knew love was a free gift he could never earn through effort or achievement. Many people came to know him as a miracle worker, but in the eyes of the world, Solanus seemed unlikely to amount to anything. He grew up on a farm and worked as a prison guard and streetcar operator, never excelling in school. He fell in love with a girl, but when he proposed, her parents were resistant. He did not know where he fit in. However, the increasing violence he saw in the world fueled a desire within him to make God's love more visible.

Experiencing the interior summons to give his life to God through the priesthood, Solanus left his family and joined the Franciscans. Despite putting all he had toward his studies, his grades suffered considerably, especially in Latin. Seeing that he could not pass the typical classes required, he was ordained what was then called a "simplex priest," with restrictions that significantly limited his ministry. Thus, after many years of grueling work and sacrifice, he was assigned the role of answering the door of the friary, a task usually given to an uneducated brother.

Fr. Solanus did not put up a fight but trusted in the unexpected way God was asking him to live his priesthood. He received each person who came with joy and interceded for them that the Lord would grant their petitions.

It was clear that Fr. Solanus had found the love that defined him. He was not concerned about what he was doing for the Lord but solely that he belonged to the Lord, who loved him unconditionally. This enabled him to trust that his "yes" to the Lord was enough. Solanus wanted this for everyone he met, and soon miracles began to happen. First dozens; then hundreds—physical cures, spiritual healings, families being reconciled, and food for the poor mysteriously showing up at the right moments.

God was able to work His mighty deeds of love through Solanus because he trusted a love that was given regardless of what he could achieve. This kind of trust opens the door of your heart to receive what is already packaged with your name on it: God's personal love for you, freely given. Trust allows us to be loved for who we are, not for what we do.

Yet, how often we project onto God our perceptions of what others have shown us. When others are disappointed with us, we can equate it with thinking that *God* is disappointed too. Or, if I don't like myself, how can God like me?

We so often think that He'll only love us when we get over that bad habit, make more time for family, let go of that grudge, etc. Yet this is nowhere in the Gospel.

When I catch myself thinking this way, I have to pause and ask myself: How did I become the judge of what God loves? How could I determine the threshold of what moves His heart?

JESUS, I TRUST IN YOU

We hear of God's initiative in the First Letter of John, that "he first loved us," prior to any of our efforts (1 John 4:19). Jesus also uses the parable of the prodigal son (Luke 15:11–32) to show the heavenly Father's gratuitous love, because He does not want us to miss out on it.

The prodigal son is a story of a father with two sons: one stays home and works with him, while the other asks for his share of the inheritance and then goes off to spend it on loose living. When this second son, the prodigal, reaches the point of destitution, he resolves to return to his father's house in hopes of being treated as a hired hand. Instead, the father runs toward him and embraces him, celebrating him as the long-lost son who is now home. At the sight of this, the older son is indignant; he does not feel appreciated by his father.

This is a parable about God the Father and the way He sees us, His children. Astonishingly, the father in the parable relates to his sons by speaking things God the Father would only say in reference to Jesus, His Son. Of the prodigal son, the father says, "[M]y son was dead, and is alive again" (Luke 15:24); and to the older son, "[Y]ou are always with me, and all that is mine is yours" (Luke 15:31). It is almost as if Jesus is in the hearts of both sons, interceding for each to go to His father, precisely at the time they least believe His love.

Neither son knew his father. The prodigal son thought he had lost his father's love because he did not earn it through obeying him; rather, he had only offended his father, not lost his love. The older son had worked hard for his father, thinking his work would earn his father's love. The father's response to each of them shows his love is far wider than their expectations.

Likewise, Jesus has won the grace for each of us to go to the Father in prayer, precisely when we least believe we are freely loved, to see how the Father sees us, to hear how He speaks to us, and to experience how He loves us in that moment. Jesus suffers when we fear to approach the Father, who is longing to embrace us. He deeply desires to see us receive the love that restores us to our dignity. He would rather risk being rejected by us than cheapen His love, downgrading it to something we could earn. He wants so much more for us. The experience of the *gift* of His love cannot be reduced.

INVITATION

- There are myriad self-help books that try to shed light on what one can do to earn love. The problem is precisely in the "self"-help part: no monologues delivered into a mirror will convince me I am loved for who I am. I need to experience through another that I am loved—not for what I can or cannot do but for who I am. Benedict XVI articulates it well: "Man comes in the profoundest sense to himself not through what he does but through what he accepts. . . . And one cannot become wholly man in any other way than by being loved, by letting oneself be loved."[1] Am I willing to admit my need for God's love?

• It is crucial to take some time every day to sit with the Lord in prayer, opening your heart to Him, as to a friend. Share with Him your desires for love and belonging, and what you think makes someone worthy of love. In the silence of your heart, let yourself be seen by Him, who loves you for your own sake—not for what you're able to do for Him in that moment, or for what you'll be able to repay Him with, but for who you are. Where have I looked to earn God's love?

• There is hardly a more tangible way to encounter the Father's unconditional love than in the Sacrament of Confession. It is here that we reveal the ways we have betrayed God and ourselves through sin, and instead of wrath and punishment, we receive His sanctifying grace. Through sin, our relationship with God, ourselves, and others is damaged. But the

[1] Joseph Ratzinger, *Introduction to Christianity*, 2nd ed. (San Francisco: Ignatius Press, 2004), 267.

grace of reconciliation given to us in Confession truly repairs those relationships. The Father waits to extend His healing, if only we come to Him freely with a contrite heart. Prepare for your next confession with an examination of conscience. When was the last time you were able to make a good confession, one you had prepared for?

From the fear that I am unlovable, deliver me, Jesus.

Through our Hope and Healing Mission for those who have suffered after abortion, my community (The Sisters of Life) has come to know a heroic woman, whom we'll call Sarah. She had many things going for her in life: a nice apartment, a good job, and a loving husband. Yet inside of her was a deep ache. In an attempt to overcome that ache, she began (in her words) "working out like a lunatic," so much so that her trainer asked her if she wanted to compete as a female bodybuilder.

When she looks back at her time as a bodybuilder, Sarah says she was literally trying to transform herself. When she would come out onto the stage, people she knew did not recognize her. Eventually, a back injury left her with lots of spare time, and she could no longer avoid reflecting on her life—most poignantly, her abortion and the decision to leave the Church decades ago. One day she googled "confession after abortion," which led her to a day retreat with our Sisters, and she later joined a woman's group to help continue her healing journey.

At one of these meetings, Sarah shared how she found out the night before that St. Margaret of Castello is the patron saint of back pain and that she had started to pray to her. To Sarah's surprise, the meeting shifted, as a relic and book on St. Margaret were on hand, and the women took turns blessing themselves and reading her story aloud.

Sarah and all those present listened to the story of how St. Margaret was rejected and totally abandoned by her parents for having a curved spine and being disabled and blind. Instead of being bitter, St. Margaret found her strength in the Lord. When people asked her how she could love so deeply after being terribly abused, she would respond, full of faith, "Oh, if you only knew what I have in my heart." Sarah began to tear up, immediately identifying with St. Margaret's parents, who had abandoned their unwanted child. She was so touched by the story that Sarah began having "Coffee with Margaret" every morning, reading more about her life and praying to this little but powerful saint. What began as a prayer to help ease back pain became far more, as through St. Margaret, Sarah experienced the forgiveness of her child lost through abortion.

God, who created us out of love, pursues our hearts like no one else, dying for us "while we were yet sinners" (Rom 5:8). Our own actions or the actions of others will never be the measure of how much we are loved or how much we can love.

If we feel unlovable, we can have the sense that something has come between God and us. We come to the false conclusion that we can't receive His love or that it's not meant for us. To feel as though we are beyond God's infinite love is an excruciating and isolating suffering. We will not believe or receive the love that is offered us, as we have shut the door to our hearts, often unknowingly.

The closing of the door to my heart is a response to something painful—something that although neither chosen or sought after, led *me* to decide I should no longer be loved. What starts off as not liking certain parts of myself can grow into self-hatred if left unchecked. And if I hate myself, the thinking follows that others should too. Yet, being loved for who we truly are is what we need most.

To claim that I am unlovable starts with the refusal to accept myself, in my humanity. My humanity reminds me that I am not God. I am not perfect, but weak, limited, and needy. This refusal of our humanity, taken to an extreme, can lead us to reject ourselves by creating a new identity that excludes or numbs the things we hate about ourselves. But cutting out or sidestepping what feels weak in us only compounds the pain and closes the door of our hearts further. Even though this kind of identity-building is championed as the road to authenticity in our culture, it is a dangerous path of destruction that is based in self-rejection.

Accepting God's unconditional love in the places of pain, in the full light of those weaknesses, allows us to embrace who we are, to our delight and surprise! Therefore, if there is a part of our history or self-image that has not been exposed to God's healing love, we'll continue to live trapped in the lie that is keeping our hearts closed.

The good news is this: whatever we are carrying does not definitively prevent us from receiving God's love. In these instances, trust gives us the courage to allow the Lord's love to see what we least like about ourselves, to encounter who we truly are, and who He truly is. It is never too late. Trust teaches us that His love makes me lovable.

JESUS, I TRUST IN YOU

As Jesus began His public ministry and encountered so many people face-to-face for the first time, His message was "repent, and believe in the gospel" (Mark 1:15). Jesus was very aware of His peoples' suffering, individually and as a nation, and had come to offer salvation. Why, then, start with such a challenge?

Repentance clears a path in the heart to receive more love. And this is what Jesus came to bring. Jesus knows that sin lies to us about who we are, and that's why He calls us to repent. When we humbly come before Him admitting our sorrow and need, repentance removes what gets in the way of receiving His love: the false conclusions of sin that we are not worthy of love or lovable.

We are all in need of repentance for our own sins. And if we have been hurt badly by the sins of others, we may need to renounce the lies those wounds inflicted on us (that I am bad and do not deserve to be loved for who I am) and the ways we have identified with them. We need to repent *because* we are lovable, because God has made us *good* at the core of our being. Repentance is allowing ourselves to be vulnerable to His healing mercy. It is a call that transforms us in order that we may truly live Jesus' words: "As the Father has loved me, so have I loved you; abide in my love" (John 15:9).

I remember reading these words of the Gospel in college and being stunned at how bold they were. How could it be? As the Father loves Jesus, Jesus loves *me*. During this time, I started to go to Eucharistic Adoration. There, in the presence of the Lord, I never knew exactly what to say, but somehow I felt like it was enough just to be there. So I kept coming back every Monday night, midnight to 1 a.m.

Adoration awakened a deep thirst within me: to be loved. And as raw as that felt, there was a consolation in acknowledging it before Him. In the stillness of the night, without being able to gather the vast expanse of my thirst in words, I knew I was upheld by His knowing presence. He simply received *me*—not because I was perfect in my own eyes or His, but because He wanted to love me. It stirred up within me the desire to orient my entire life to God and let go of what was holding me back from Him.

God knows one way of loving: totally. And it raises hearts to life again.

INVITATION

- Many of us go through our days unknowingly agreeing to lies about not being worthy of love, falsely confirming their validity again and again. Ask the Lord for light to see where you doubt your God-given goodness. Am I aware of what makes me feel least worthy of love?

- The places we do not feel worthy of love are places we have shut the doors of our hearts. We need God's healing love to speak the truth of our goodness. Are we willing to ask the Lord to show us His love, which runs far deeper than our weaknesses, in these trying moments of our daily lives? He may show you that there is an underlying reason for your mistrust of His love for you—maybe a painful betrayal or sin. Is there something in my life that brings me away from God's love? Where is the Lord inviting me to repent?

• Spend some time in the presence of Jesus in the Eucharist, the one place where each of us is totally received. Tell Him the parts you can't accept about yourself, as this is what inhibits you from believing in the unconditional love He offers. Unconditional love does not mean that God approves of my sins; but as His child I am totally received, and He is drawing me to freedom in grace. In His gaze I am not abandoned or rejected. Am I running from a deep ache in my heart by trying to transform myself into an image I like?

Day 3

From the false security that
I have what it takes,
deliver me, Jesus.

When the young shepherd David single-handedly ran
to meet his opponent, Goliath, the whole destiny of
the Israelite army depended on whether he had what it
took to defeat the colossal Philistine warrior.

David, however, did not have confidence in himself
or in the battle gear given to him. He took off the armor
and approached Goliath, saying, "You come to me with
a sword and with a spear . . . ; but I come to you in the
name of the LORD of hosts, the God of the armies of
Israel" (1 Sam 17:45). David had confidence in God,
who had called him to witness His power to the Philis-
tines. So, with his sling and stone, he defeated Goliath.
And David would learn many times throughout his
life that he could rest in God's strength, not his own
capacities.

Trust is not merely believing God can accomplish
what He is asking of me, but that He *will* do what He is
asking in and through me.

After years of being matchless on the battlefield,
David was tempted to be comfortable in his abilities
and judgement. When he took another man's wife to

be his own and purposefully had that man killed, David realized he was far from relying on God. He repented, and in asking the Lord for mercy, David states that a burnt offering of an animal is not what God wants, but the "sacrifice acceptable to God is a broken spirit; a broken and contrite heart, O God, you will not despise" (Ps 51:17). The battle God was trying to win in David all along was for David's trust—the battle of self-reliance vs. God-reliance. Ironically, David would learn that our misery gives us the greatest access to God's heart, if we trust in His mercy. God allows His heart to be moved, to be "conquered," by the slightest indication of our repentance.

A young woman who entered Carmel at age fifteen also had her own battle to fight against self-reliance: St. Therese. Her one goal was to become a saint, but she quickly found that she was completely incapable of achieving it on her own. There were so many virtues to acquire and sacrifices to be made. She felt she was too weak. However, everything she knew of God was rooted in the truth that He would not inspire a desire that was impossible. Therefore sanctity was not about what she could do for God, or about stacking up her own salvation points, but rather boldly believing in His love, trusting He would supply what she lacked.

Therese would employ a new tactic against self-reliance. When a moment came where she needed patience, or another virtue, even though she did not feel she had it in her, she would ask it from the Lord, and step into the situation with confidence that He would provide it. And He did, as no situation was too big or too small for Him. From a human perspective, this is a very vulnerable way to live, precisely because it does not seek security in oneself. It is the sure way to live the union of love with God, which is holiness. Her trust in the midst of her "littleness" gave her the conviction to cast aside all self-reliance, saying to the Lord, "In the evening of this life, I shall appear before You with empty hands."[1] Trust stands only in the security of His love.

A lack of security in myself is not a mistake nor a reason for shame. When paired with a bold confidence in the Lord, it is a sign of spiritual health. It helps me to put my security in someone greater—the Lord. If we believe that we have what it takes, we box God out of the picture. So we shouldn't be surprised if, in His mercy, God may allow us to fall on occasion so that we can come to rely on Him more fully.

JESUS, I TRUST IN YOU

Returning to the town He grew up in, Jesus entered the synagogue in Nazareth. He was handed the scroll of Isaiah, and read aloud, "The Spirit of the Lord is upon me, because he has anointed me to preach good news to the poor. He has sent me to proclaim release to the captives and recovering of sight to the blind, to set at liberty those who are oppressed" (Luke 4:18). As everyone looked at Him, Jesus closed the scroll and announced that this prophetic word was that day "fulfilled in your hearing" (v. 21).

We are the poor, the captive, the blind, the oppressed

---

[1] St. Thérèse of Lisieux, "Act of Oblation to Merciful Love," in *Story of a Soul*, trans. John Clarke, 3rd ed. (Washington, DC: ICS, 1996), 277.

ones that Jesus spoke of. With Him, our standards of success—being competent and perfect—have no weight. Jesus, the Anointed One, upholds us in our need.

Jesus Himself also lives what He shares with us: a life of utter reliance. It would be quite easy to assume that Jesus, of all people, should have lived self-sufficiently. But He did, and does, *nothing* without the Father. "Truly, truly, I say to you, the Son can do nothing of his own accord, but only what he sees the Father doing; for whatever he does, that the Son does likewise" (John 5:19). Jesus' actions were continually inspired by and united to those of the Father. He is not a God who is isolated and competitive, but one who chooses to do nothing alone. Jesus was not ashamed of this but proclaimed it.

As Jesus invited His followers, so He invites each one of us into this sturdy love between the Father and Him so that we too can live as He does. We know that the love between the Father and the Son is the Holy Spirit. Jesus told the apostles, "But the Counselor, the Holy Spirit, whom the Father will send in my name, he will teach you all things" (John 14:26); and also, "[H]e dwells with you, and will be in you" (John 14:17). Jesus desires to impart to us the Holy Spirit, that we would receive and live in the very security of His unchanging love. For those who open themselves to this Spirit of Love, their ordinary lives become imbued with the brilliance of relying on God. Our intrinsic lack becomes our greatest treasure when we allow ourselves to be anointed and filled by His divine life.

INVITATION

- Share with someone you trust an area of weakness that you have not been able to conquer with your own strength, asking them to support you in prayer. Confession is an irreplaceable source of grace; however, having someone to hold you accountable can be a way to step into that sacramental strength. This can dismantle some of the pride that makes us willfully independent.

- Jesus does not expect us to have what it takes. That's why He came to save us and is honored to be our rock of security. We need the Lord and those He sends us. Even the most seraphic saints needed spiritual directors. Where is it hardest for me to receive help? Typically, the places where we feel most competent, and conversely where we are embarrassed by our lack of capability, are where we are tempted to cut others out. Instead of baptizing our perfectionism by leaning on our own strength, will we move God's heart by trusting He is our security?

- When you are applauded for a job well done or, on the contrary, when you are frustrated with your own inadequacy, can you pause to praise God for securing your identity in His love and not in what you can or can't do? Before beginning a project, responding to an email, or answering a question, simply pray, "Come, Holy Spirit." This practice forms a steady reliance on Him for light and direction.

DAY 4

From the fear that trusting You will leave me more destitute, deliver me, Jesus.

Although we may have never said it aloud, many of us have likely prayed, in one way or another, "Lord, I want to be close to you, but not too close."

Skimming the stories of any number of saints can give the impression that their lives were all about suffering. St. John of the Cross was thrown into a basement cell and banished by his own community. St. Thomas More was put to death for speaking the truth about the sacredness of marriage. St. Joan of Arc was burned at the stake. Padre Pio was given the stigmata, bearing on his body the five wounds of Christ.

Thinking about these saints and others, we might begin to wonder, "So if I really go out on a limb for You, Lord, and trust You, will I be worse off for it? Does loving You mean I will be left destitute, to face life without even the necessities?"

St. Thomas More's friend of thirty-five years, the scholar Erasmus, said of him, "He was one of the happiest men that ever I met."[1] And Padre Pio would surprisingly say, "I really cannot tell you how grateful I

---

[1] Aloysius Roche, *A Bedside Book of Saints* (Milwaukee: Bruce, 1934), 44.

am to so tender a Father for the many benefits He continues to lavish on us."[2]

In reality, saints had a joy deeper than passing feelings or external circumstances, because their entire lives were consumed by love. A saint is someone who loves God with their whole heart. The person who has been in love knows that a sacrifice for their beloved is different than a sacrifice for someone they detest. In fact, they would *willingly* suffer to spare the one they love pain, or simply to be with them. Therefore, in the suffering they endured, the saints could say with Christ, "No one takes [my life] from me, but I lay it down of my own accord" (John 10:18). Love alone gives meaning to suffering, and the love of Christ turns even the direst circumstances into eternal gain.

When we become invested in something or someone, it hurts all the more when it is taken from us or we fail to find what we hoped for. We're tempted to think it would have been better if we never began to walk down this path in the first place, feeling like our trust is broken because we did not agree to this. Yet, God would never pull the rug out from under us. He has only one intention: to never be separated from us. Jesus does allow us to be stripped of things, even good things, that keep us from closer union with Him, so as to clothe us with Himself. We are emptied only to receive more of Him.

In 1964, on the small island of Okinawa, which is off the coast of Japan, a Navy chaplain found himself

2 St. Pio of Pietrelcina, *Letter Vol. II: Correspondence with Raffaelina Cearse, Noblewoman (1914–1915)*, ed. Melchiorre of Pobladura, Alessandro of Ripabottoni, and Father Gerardo Di Flumeri, trans. Mary F. Ingoldsby (Foggia, IT: Edizioni "Padre Pio de Pietrelcina," 1987), 277.

entrusted with the spiritual welfare of thousands of men preparing to be sent into Vietnam during the war.

The island air was heavy with fear and anxiety. Men who were away from their families faced countless temptations. At the same time, this priest who had been assigned to care for these men began to experience a deep interior emptiness. As he started to question his faith, he wondered how this could be happening to him, as he had tried so hard to be a good priest and to faithfully serve God. He wondered if the most fitting thing that could happen to him would be to die with his troops. The words that came to the surface of his heart over and over again were Christ's words on the Cross: "My God, my God, why have you forsaken me?" (Ps 22:1). Despite the overwhelming emptiness he felt, the chaplain continued night after night to go to the tin-hut chapel on base and sit before the tabernacle.

Every day he chose again to be a spiritual father to his troops, celebrating Mass, hearing confessions, encouraging his men, and organizing retreats for them. The last of the six retreats at Okinawa in those months had the commanding general and most of the senior officers of the base in attendance. His choice to be faithful to a deeper love—his commitment to Christ—rather than escaping its difficulty bore tremendous fruit. Then one day, the desolation lifted completely. In the months that followed, the priest would volunteer to follow his men into Vietnam, continuing to bring them Christ in the midst of war. The commanding general, Lewis Walt, reported, "No single individual in this command contributed more to the morale of the individual Marine here in Vietnam than Father O'Connor."³

Chaplain John O'Connor, who would later become Cardinal O'Connor, took the narrow gate of a faithful love which leads to life (Matt 7:13–14). He trusted the path of God in his emptiness, and through him God filled countless hearts. Trust carves out a greater capacity for love within us.

JESUS, I TRUST IN YOU

St. Paul, in his letter to the Philippians, writes of Christ, " . . . though he was in the form of God, [Jesus] did not count equality with God a thing to be grasped, but emptied himself, taking the form of a servant, being born in the likeness of men" (Phil 2:6–7). Jesus divested Himself of His power, emptied Himself to become man. Stripped of His divine plentitude, His self-emptying is a gift for us.

We will never be able to fully comprehend what this act of humility was for Jesus, in Him becoming man. Jesus does not hold His love back from us, nor does He calculate if some of it is not received or treasured. Even in heaven we will never be able to sufficiently appreciate it!

Jesus Himself said to His disciples on the eve of His death, "I will not leave you desolate; I will come to you" (John 14:18). Knowing that they will feel abandoned after His death, He speaks directly into their fear. Not only does He give them His presence in the Eucharist and the promise of the Holy Spirit that same

---

³ Lewis W. Walt, Legion of Merit report for Chaplain O'Connor, August 29, 1965.

night, but He also offers them a new invitation to intimacy, precisely in this hungry place of their hearts that is experienced as emptiness. " . . . you will weep and lament, but the world will rejoice; you will be sorrowful, but your sorrow will turn into joy" (John 16:20). Comparing the aching of our hearts for His new life to a woman in childbirth, Jesus wants us to see its transitory yet fruitful nature. He continues, "So you have sorrow now, but I will see you again and your hearts will rejoice, and no one will take your joy from you" (John 16:22). Just as Jesus' emptying brought deeper love, so too will our willingness to be emptied for His sake be a way to receive His love.

INVITATION

- We need not be alarmed when, in the course of our career, ministry, or vocation, we experience times of emptiness, like Chaplain O'Connor. Of course, we can feel empty inside when we have walked away from the Lord through serious sin, but if that is not the case, it may be that Jesus is stretching your heart to allow you to receive more of what He came to share: His divinity. This experience, which feels like a loss, can be an invitation to love with His heart, and to experience in a small way what He did in becoming man for our sake. Have you experienced emptiness that proved to be an invitation to more?

- Genuine prayer empties us of ourselves, turning

our focus on Him and those around us whom He asks us to love. When we feel empty inside during prayer, and we do not necessarily know what to say or are tempted to fill the space with self-focused thoughts, we can simply call on Him, bring to mind short verses from Scripture, or sit in a loving awareness of Him. Emptiness, when given to Jesus, is a prayer in itself. What are the thoughts that tend to distract me during prayer? Can I learn to recognize them and direct my attention back to the Lord?

- During the inevitable times of interior emptiness in our relationship with the Lord, we are easily tempted to change our path or to walk away from Him. It is common to think about discontinuing our prayer or withdrawing from activities that feed our souls and serve others. But "in times of desolation, never make a change" to spiritual commitments, for this is not the time to make changes in our routine.[4] Look at the heroic acts of fidelity that you continue to live, however small they may be, as rays of God's love bringing light into the world. A way to be faithful to the Lord during this is to remain in prayer for a set time, regardless of it being consoling or dry. When you are tempted to leave early, resist and reject the temptation by staying a minute longer than originally planned.

---

[4] Timothy M. Gallagher, *The Discernment of Spirits: An Ignatian Guide for Everyday Living* (New York: Crossroads, 2005), 74.

DAY 5

From all suspicion of Your words and promises, deliver me, Jesus.

Words have immense power. And when backed by actions, they can have an even greater weight. They can chart the course of our life and happiness, or threaten our destruction.

One of the greatest Church Fathers, St. Augustine, said, "To believe what you please, and not to believe what you please, is to believe yourselves and not the gospel."[1] He speaks from experience. For years St. Augustine skirted the moral teachings of Christ because he knew Christ opposed the life of sin he was clinging to. Following Christ, to Augustine, meant forfeiting his humanity—or so he thought.

Centuries later, many people still believe that the calling to which Jesus invites us is too high for us, or that His words are too good to be true. Each of us, like Augustine, is faced with a decision to make about Jesus. Are we open to what He says? Pilate listened to Jesus speak that Good Friday morning and was not able to recognize who it was standing before him—Almighty God. Thinking his position as governor was at stake, Pilate's judgement was clouded by the desire to do what he wanted, regardless of whether Jesus was innocent or

[1] St. Augustine, *Contra Faustum*, 17.3.

not. How common it is to put God on trial because of our own doubt in His promises.

St. Monica, however, clung in faith to God's word that her prayers for the conversion of her son, St. Augustine, would be answered. For Augustine, the idea of happiness revolved around his mistress, honors, and wealth. But the witness of Christians he encountered led him to reconsider what was important to him.

He spent most of his search debating rather than listening, until one day, God very clearly stepped in. While in the height of his struggle to surrender to what was becoming more and more clear, he heard a mysterious voice say, "Take up and read."[2] Picking up the Scriptures, Augustine opened up to Romans 13:14: "But put on the Lord Jesus Christ, and make no provision for the flesh, to gratify its desires." This left no doubt in his heart that God had heard his anguish and was speaking to him directly. God's word was alive and, in fact, directing him to a life free of slavery to sexual sin, which he had not thought possible up until then.

After experiencing that God's word could be trusted, St. Augustine fully embraced the faith, and few have written so many words to testify of their trust in God's word. His extensive writings were critical in shaping how the Church interpreted Scripture and have guided countless hearts to make the Lord's words their own. Like St. Augustine, may we too live this trust, by looking at Jesus to be the standard by which we judge the world. For St. Augustine, serving God became his soul's freedom and delight. Trust is being ready to accept the Lord's words simply because they are His.

[2] Augustine, *Confessions*, 8.12.29.

Even when we do not fully understand, a trusting heart can proclaim to Jesus, "Lord, to whom shall we go? You have the words of eternal life" (John 6:68).

JESUS, I TRUST IN YOU

A centurion sent elders to Jesus to request He come and heal his dying servant. As Jesus went with them, another group arrived with an updated message. The centurion wished to tell Jesus, "Lord, do not trouble yourself, for I am not worthy to have you come under my roof. . . . But say the word, and let my servant be healed" (Luke 7:6–7). Jesus "marveled" at this man (v. 9), for the centurion had revealed his belief in the power of Jesus' word. If Jesus said the word, it would happen. The force of Jesus' word, to this centurion, was attached to who he believed Jesus was.

For us, it's upsetting when someone doesn't trust what we say, even if it's something small, such as telling a family member we've locked the front door, and then watching them go over to check it. Even more so, it's painful when we share something of greater significance, such as how devastated we were by a certain situation, only to hear our story questioned. When others do not trust our words and promises, we realize they do not trust *us*. Jesus' words and promises are likewise bound up with Him, so that in receiving them, one receives *Him*. He is the Word, spoken by the Father, revealing who the Father is (John 1:1, 18); and whoever receives Him, receives the Father (Matt 10:40).

God's words and promises are manifold, but one

excerpt of Jesus' words from Scripture sums up many: "I am the way, and the truth, and the life" (John 14:6). His words proclaim that He is what our hearts are looking for, and that nothing in this world can take Him away from us, if we so accept Him. To emphasize the importance of the truths He was sharing throughout Scripture, He would start by saying, "Truly, truly, I say to you." Jesus longed to be heard and believed. When he was put on trial for what He proclaimed, Jesus had multiple opportunities to explain Himself differently or go back on what He said before Pilate. But by embracing His death, He profoundly showed us that He means what He says.

Jesus loves sincerity, naming it as a sign of a true disciple (John 1:47). Therefore He does not exaggerate, for He realizes it is hard to trust someone who often stretches their words. And He does not lie. There is a vulnerability in simply relaying things as they are. He knows who He is and is not trying to sell us anything.

By sharing Himself with us, Jesus trusts us and takes the risk that He will not be believed or respected. For the sake of giving all an opportunity to hear Him, He suffers the pain of having people twist His words and do things in His name that He does not stand for. Despite this, to Him we are still worth trusting, in the hope of arousing our hearts to trust Him in return.

INVITATION

- *Take up and read.* Do I know what Jesus says? St. Augustine recommended praying to the Lord for understanding when we are struggling with His word.

As Christians, each of us should be spending time soaking in the Lord's word, especially in the Gospels and in the teachings of Christ that we least understand. Ask the Lord to reveal His love for you in His words. And then, even before understanding clicks, take that leap, as St. Augustine did, to start living according to His word. "Understanding is the reward of faith. Therefore, seek not to understand that you may believe, but believe that you may understand."[3]

- Recognize that there is *power* in God's word. In Genesis, in the creation of the world, He spoke and it came to be. Therefore, take an honest look at the standards you live by: when you want to do something you know is wrong, do you decide that the Lord's standard is wrong, and excuse yourself? Speak to God about what you really want, are looking for, and feel afraid He won't supply.

- Although the creation of the world began long ago, it continues with each new life. God intended me to exist, and breathed His life into me. When I struggle to believe God's word, it is good to recognize that I am a *word* spoken by God. Sit in this truth: *He spoke and I came to be.*

---

[3] Augustine, *Tractates on the Gospel of John*, 29.6.

Day 6

From the rebellion against
childlike dependency on You,
deliver me, Jesus.

Few people in history have been known for their zeal
and pursuit of excellence as much as Saul of Tarsus. He
was a strict observer of the Jewish law, attesting that he
"persecuted the Church of God violently and tried to
destroy it; . . . so extremely zealous was I for the tradi-
tions of my fathers" (Gal 1:13–14).

But one day, while on his way to imprison more
Christians, a blinding light knocked him over and
enveloped him. He heard a voice say, "Saul, Saul, why
do you persecute me?" (Acts 26:14). It was Jesus, who
bid Saul to help others "turn from darkness to light" by
placing their faith in Him (v. 18).

With this new mission, Saul became Paul. He no
longer had righteousness in himself, but he could now
claim a new sonship: "for in Christ Jesus you are all sons
of God, through faith" (Gal 3:26). Instead of continuing
to take matters into his own hands—which all rebellion
does—Paul sought to receive what the Father wanted to
provide.

Finding reason to rejoice in all situations, he wrote,
"[F]or I have learned, in whatever state I am, to be

content. I know how to be abased, and I know how to abound; in any and all circumstances I have learned the secret of facing plenty and hunger, abundance and want" (Phil 4:11–12). It did not matter if he was shipwrecked, stoned, beaten, threatened, or persecuted; he knew his filial status and that gave him the freedom to daringly proclaim the truth he had learned, thereby converting and healing multitudes. Paul was anchored in his eternal inheritance, assuring those he brought to faith, "God has sent the Spirit of his Son into our hearts, crying, 'Abba! Father!' So through God you are no longer a slave but a son, and if a son then an heir" (Gal 4:6–7).

Paul was freed from the self-defeating autonomy that began in Eden. In the garden of Eden, Adam and Eve were given an abundance of beauty, nourishment, and peace. The only restriction was that at the very center of the garden was a tree, in which they were asked not to eat its fruit, or they would die. The *Catechism* puts forth Adam and Eve's choice to eat the fruit: "Man, tempted by the devil, let his trust in his Creator die in his heart and, abusing his freedom, disobeyed God's command.... All subsequent sin would be disobedience toward God and lack of trust in his goodness" (CCC 397). It's not an unfamiliar story to a single soul. All of us have a decision to make at the very center of our being—a choice to trust God or to grasp for what we do not think He will provide. The choice for trust, far from crushing our vitality, brings a new Eden to life, where we can live in the freedom of the children of God.

Now, people may not initially see childlike dependency as a sign of strength or courage, but it is what gave St. Paul his boldness. The world equates children with naivete and silliness. However, those are the features of child*ish*ness, which is not our aim. Child*ish*ness demands that everything is done on my terms, rather than at the direction of the one who knows best what I need. Only one who is mature in the spiritual life sees the power that lies in receptivity. "But to all who received him, who believed in his name, he gave power to become children of God; who were born, not of blood nor of the will of the flesh nor of the will of man, but of God" (John 1:12–13).

Childlike dependency means being flexible when circumstances change in my day, because I know God is in charge. It means genuine delight in the smallest joys because I know they are a gift from Him and are not owed to me. It means a freedom from fear, which allows me to face my limits with every expectation of the Father's blessing.

I have one word taped to the inside of the laptop I use: *ASK*. It's not intended as a threat for other users but is a simple reminder to me that I need to ask the Lord for help throughout my day, whatever my tasks are. It is a way to stay close to Him instead of running ahead on my own. And I've seen His faithfulness.

The word "ASK" reminds us to *ask for help to receive* what He provides and to not fend for ourselves. I'm not as conscious of that faded little sign anymore, because what began as a reminder to lean on Christ in the midst of my work has opened my heart to seek Him wherever I am. And far from being child*ish*, it has all the thrust of heaven. Trust enables us to receive the providential care of God in all things.

JESUS, I TRUST IN YOU

After Adam and Eve ate the fruit, God did not walk away. He came to them, knowing He would never leave them. Yet, what would remedy the rift between them, rescuing them from the consequence of death they now carried?

"For God so loved the world that he gave his only-begotten Son, that whoever believes in him should not perish but have eternal life" (John 3:16). *He gave His Son.* This is the heavenly Father we trust. God wants us to believe in His goodness, knowing the conviction of His goodness opens our hearts to truly live our dependence on Him with freedom, joy, and peace.

Through the gift of the Son, Jesus, we see the privilege of what it means to live as a child of the Father. The Father is continually pouring His life into Jesus, His Son. In various ways, Jesus would proclaim, "I and the Father are one" (John 10:30). For Jesus, the daily dependency on the Father, in which He chose to live His earthly life, was not a burden to be surmounted but a love He was inviting us into.

As the Father gave His Son, the Son leads us to the Father. Even the best of earthly friends do not share their father with you to be your own. Jesus gives us this unspeakable privilege so that we could truly say with Him, "*Our* Father" (Matt 6:9, emphasis added). Jesus wants to give us that which is most valuable to Him, that we would each come to know His Father truly as *my* Father.

"Let the children come to me, and do not hinder them; for to such belongs the kingdom of God. Truly,

I say to you, whoever does not receive the kingdom of God like a child shall not enter it" (Luke 18:16–17). It is as though Jesus says to each one of us, no matter where we are, "The path I have for you is simple enough for a child to follow." When we know we are loved as His very own, the Lord's way is wholly uncomplicated.

INVITATION

• Find a way to help remind yourself to ASK for help to receive what He wants to provide—perhaps a note on the mirror, fridge, or dashboard. By inviting us to pray, "Give us this day our daily bread," the Lord wants to have the opportunity to show you His goodness (see CCC 2828).

• Our God is the God of heaven and earth, manifesting His love at times through healings, conversions, and Eucharistic miracles. The heart of a child readily believes He is capable and desirous of moving mountains in our lives. In the places we are tempted to be cynical about our faith and relationship with God, can we ask for the heart of a child, which is truly open to receive what He gives? Do I pray to God with a filial boldness?

• If pain defined our early years, anything that has the scent of dependency can carry with it the sting of negativity. It takes courage to receive, to learn to trust when it has been broken. Jesus told us, "[F]or the Father himself loves you" (John 16:27). In the times when we are overwhelmed or feel that life is too complicated, ask God to reveal to you His fatherhood. Do I desire a renewed sense of what it truly means to be a child? Where is God inviting me to a greater dependence on Him?

From refusals and reluctances in accepting Your will, deliver me, Jesus.

With its heartrending beginning, the Old Testament story of Joseph and his eleven brothers is one of my favorites. Joseph is disliked by his brothers not only for being preferred by their father but because Joseph recounts his dreams of them bowing down before him. Fueled by jealous anger, his brothers plot to kill Joseph.

Providentially, they catch sight of a passing caravan and are persuaded to sell him as a slave instead. It's hard to imagine the anguish Joseph must have felt on that agonizing journey to Egypt. He was immersed in a people whose language he did not speak, headed to a distant place that was completely foreign, and grappling in his heart with the immense betrayal of his brothers. What were his thoughts as, every minute, he was separated more and more from the only life he had ever known, now destined to a life of slavery?

God does not will evil. God does not want anyone to be sold into slavery; rather, it pains Him to see someone suffer. God does *allow* evil—but He allows it to bring about a greater good than if it hadn't happened at all. The difficulty is that we don't see that good initially, or perhaps for many years. We may not see it at all until the Lord shows it to us on the other side of this life—after we die.

Joseph would never have guessed where his new life, which at first felt like a death, would bring him. He could have easily become bitter and resentful, but at some point he chose to trust God in those painful circumstances of his life. Scripture tells us that he continued to be faithful to the Lord throughout his years as a slave, even when unjustly imprisoned.

As He always is, God was at work, crafting an amazing story of triumph. Through Joseph's surrender in trust to a plan that he did not understand or see the good in, he gave God permission to accomplish *His* plan. As the years went by, Joseph saw the faithfulness of God, who revealed to him an oncoming famine and placed him in Pharaoh's service to oversee the storehouses of grain. Seeing his brothers arrive in Egypt and kneel before him to beg for grain for their kindred, Joseph began to understand. It was not about vengeance or power—no. He saw, through his brothers' evil plan of years ago, a creative God who, without limiting our freedom, could bring abundant blessing.

Overcome with emotion, Joseph looked upon his brothers, telling them what he had learned: "As for you, you meant evil against me; but God meant it for good, to bring it about that many people should be kept alive, as they are today" (Gen 50:20).

God meant it for good. Joseph's acceptance of God's mysterious will saved thousands during the years of the famine, including his brother Judah, from whose line St. Joseph, the foster father of Jesus, would be born. God so revered Joseph's trust that it would become a foreshadowing of His own Son's exile to Egypt as a part of His mission.

We too can wrestle to perceive God's will at work in our lives. The human heart often seeks to comprehend before it can submit. And yet how often it is only in hindsight that we can see with His infinite wisdom! Trust knows that God always intends my good.

JESUS, I TRUST IN YOU

The Gospels tell us that in the garden of Gethsemane, Jesus fell on his face while praying, "My Father, if it be possible, let this chalice pass from me; nevertheless, not as I will, but as you will" (Matt 26:39). What were those moments like for Jesus?

Here Jesus finds Himself alone, standing before the weight of the sins of the world, and the tremendous love within Him. Jesus' love is far vaster than all the evil throughout all of time. Yet, the Father's plan for Jesus to suffer, die, and rise on the third day did not result in everyone accepting the eternal salvation won for them. This is torturous for His heart, which aches for each human soul. In fact, the immense outpouring of His love will only worsen the pain of those who will reject Him. Being separated from one person we love, even temporarily, is difficult; even so, it is hard for us to imagine the magnitude of Jesus' sorrow at the thought of losing many loved ones forever.

In light of all this, Jesus says "yes." He consents to the Father's plan, trusting that because it is the Father's plan, it will bear the most fruit. More than holding onto thoughts of what "should" be, Jesus desires what the Father desires.

God's will is a plan to bring us into union with Him and is always a wellspring of new life. He wonders if a heart will love Him for His own sake, even when the path is different than they intended. Are we only loving Him, trusting Him, because we've liked or understood everything so far? He longs to be loved not for what He does but for who He is. God knows that by inviting us into living a selfless love, we can begin to live His will, which is most true to our dignity while creating a deep intimacy with Him.

INVITATION

- In varying ways, we can find ourselves in the spiritual journey of Joseph. If grappling to surrender is where you are, give yourself the space to be in the caravan, like Joseph, and keep an open dialogue with the Lord. Is there a current circumstance or event that you are struggling to see good in? Even before you are convinced that *He means it for good*, make an act of faith, saying in your own words, "God is present here, and has a good plan for me, especially in the unknown."

- Little did Joseph know that the very thing that seemed to shatter his dreams was becoming the pathway to them. Ask for the grace to let go of your plans, which may be good but could limit

God's plan for you. When we say "yes" to God's will in our lives, our hearts become free to let Him unfold His unforeseen but loving design.

- *Thy will be done.* This union of my will with God's will is powerful beyond compare! Jesus spoke strongly of it, as He told His disciples, "My food is to do the will of him who sent me" (John 4:34). It was what nourished and strengthened Him. Living united to God in His will for us, He mysteriously puts us, as it were, in charge of the "storehouses of grace," that our love may go out to feed a world desperate for love. Where have you seen God's faithfulness revealed in situations that turned out differently than you planned?

Day 8

From anxiety about the future,
deliver me, Jesus.

In the 1930s, a young couple fell deeply in love. Soon after, the young woman found out she was diagnosed with tuberculosis, which was considered incurable and deadly at the time. She decided to sever all contact with the young man, without telling him her reasons, knowing this news would grieve him. As difficult as this was for her, she wanted a full future for him.

Over the next several years, her condition worsened, yet her faith grew tremendously in her suffering. Her family brought her to the holy priest Solanus Casey in hopes of being cured, as the Lord was working miracles through him. The friar asked her, "Is God asking too much of you?" Pausing thoughtfully, she replied, "No." By the following day, she was healed. Shortly after, and ten years after their split, she reached out to the young man she had been in love with, only to hear him admit that he had never been able to love another.

Is God asking too much? This young woman could have said, "Yes—my dreams, my future, the difficulties for me and my family!" But she had come to know the gift of her faith so much more deeply in her suffering and in her estimation that it was all worth it. What could be lost if she had found the treasure that nothing

51

could diminish? Faith had shifted her priorities to put God above all else, even her own wants and those of her family. This act of trust allowed her to face the future in peace.

We all have real needs, and we encounter real difficulties in obtaining them. Some planning and thinking ahead is prudent, but first and foremost we need to inquire, "What does God have planned for me?" We hear Jesus say that in the same way a builder should assess if there are ample supplies to complete his project, and a king should take counsel to decide if his troops are adequate for defeating the enemy, so too we must take stock of what is necessary if we wish to follow Him: namely, to be ready to renounce all for His sake (Luke 14:25–33). His description of true prudence is bold. As the *Catechism* tells us, prudence helps us "to discern our true good in every circumstance and to choose the right means of achieving it" (CCC 1806).

The young woman with tuberculosis knew that Jesus is our true good and that it is a false prudence that makes pleasing ourselves or others the highest good. She loved life and those around her, but chose Christ as her priority and put the future, with all its uncertainties, securely in His Hands. She began to trust Him, that whatever this sickness entailed, He had her best interest in mind.

Most of us are masters at running ahead to think of the worst-case scenario. Yet we cannot know what the future holds, and the grace to live it will only be given in the moment. The temptation to focus on ourselves will lead us down the wrong path; it makes us lose sight of God. Without seeking to follow Him, I forge onward—

stressed and alone—convinced no one is looking out for me.

How do we live with trust regarding the future? Trust is looking at the days and years ahead as the unraveling of the gift of my life for Jesus. And at the end of my life, I will have given it all back to Him. Of course, Jesus is not asking us to die without a house, a closet of clothes, friends and family, or a bank account. But whatever we are given is meant to be given back to Him so that it does not take us away from loving Him. He is first in our lives. And in the promise of heaven, we receive an exponential, overflowing bounty from our gift to Him: the fullness of His life.

My religious community is quite indebted to the young couple who entrusted their future to the Lord—that they surrendered to the Lord's perfect timing. They went on to have eight children, one being Mother Agnes Mary, the first Superior General of the Sisters of Life.

JESUS, I TRUST IN YOU

Every year at Christmas, as we look into the manger scene, we are reminded of the simple yet profound truth of the Incarnation. We marvel that baby Jesus opened His human eyes to follow time and reside in space! If He who created time and space chose to willingly submit to it, may we likewise see the richness He found in it.

To human eyes, it may seem as though no one planned out the details for Jesus' debut that wintry night, so primitive were the provisions. With thousands of years foretelling His coming through the prophets, was there no spare room to house Him? Could not He who aligned the stars perfectly that night have planned things better than to have His Son born amidst stable animals in a stranger's backyard?

Joseph and Mary, newly entrusted with raising the Son of God, would have been tempted to feel the weight of procuring the perfect place for Jesus' birth. But to be anxious was not part of their entrustment. Nor is it ours. Their focus that night—as it would be for the rest of time—was receiving the eternal love of the Father, moment by moment. The trust in the hearts of Joseph and Mary was in fact the perfect place for Jesus' birth, as the Father intended.

Our Father knew far too many of His children would be born in circumstances that seemed unprepared or unintended. In His goodness, the Father wanted no one to think the external circumstances had any bearing on their value. Through Jesus' humble birth, the Father made plainly evident what really matters: rejoicing in the new life given! Each child that exists is proof of the Father's planning.

From the moment of His birth, Jesus invited us to set our hearts on things above, not in what "moth and rust consume" (Matt 6:19). Our future lies in eternity, which is our only goal. The treasure of time, which Jesus jumped into so readily, is that it invites us to begin to receive eternity now.

INVITATION

- Speaking of how easy it may be to worry about our needs, what we are to eat and what we are to wear, Jesus says, "[Y]our heavenly Father knows that you need them all. But seek first his kingdom and his righteousness, and all these things shall be yours as well" (Matt 6:32–33). We know that we cannot control the future; but at the same time, we have desires and needs on the road ahead. What we can plan for, no matter what, is making our relationship with God a priority. He will honor that greatly, helping us to recognize that the gift of time set aside in prayer *is* our tangible act of trust in Him. In my busy schedule, do I make time every day for prayer?

- *Is God asking too much?* God does not want us to fear the future. When I catch myself in a negative spiral of thoughts about the future, can I remember He is only asking me to live *today*? To love *today*? To suffer what is difficult, to savor what is a joy, only for *today*, for love of Him? What triggers worry in my day to day living? While many things can affect my future, nothing can take away my eternal future. What am I scared of losing in the future?

- God often has us begin following Him before we know where we are going, and He builds upon it. He desires us to be faithful to the inspirations that come, one at a time, even if they do not seem intuitive. As the master architect, He does not want us spending hours of our life stressed, planning for things that may never happen, and grieving over things we may never lose. The unexpected arises in all of our lives, but our preparation is *trust*— just like Joseph and Mary received Jesus on that Christmas night. Can I recognize the immediate next step, even if I cannot see the full plans of the future?

DAY 9

From resentment or excessive preoccupation with the past, deliver me, Jesus.

We all have times in our lives that we would love to go back and relive differently—that relationship I did not fully appreciate at the time, that failed opportunity at work, losing that championship game from senior year. Often it's not just a sorrow that keeps our hearts going back in time but a nostalgia for a lost joy.

Whether we are frustrated that we can't reclaim what is no longer or are tired of our ongoing regret, the finality of the past can consume us if we do not believe in a God who is outside of time. To Him it looks different. Not only does He hold our past, but He can also show us His mysterious and transformative presence even there. And it is only in the light of eternity that we'll have a clear vision of His designs in our life.

Thankfully, we share some of His timeless quality, as we hunger for an everlasting joy. Life here below falls short of our desires, yet our dissatisfactions—small or large—matter. They point us toward the Eternal One.

A famous actress in France, Eve Lavalliere, was at the height of her career in the early 1900s. Her fame and fortune were the envy of Paris, and European royalty sought her performances. Offstage she was surrounded by men, parties, and acclaim. But Eve was terribly lonely. She said, "A voice seemed to follow me everywhere saying: 'Eve, you weren't made for this sort of thing.'"[1]

The pain of Eve's childhood had left her with a thirst for love and meaning that she would only discover the fulfillment of many years later. As a teen she had witnessed her father shoot her mother and then take his own life. Escaping from her house that dreadful day, she never saw her one brother again. She left everything behind and sought to make a new life for herself in the theater.

Her success never settled her broken heart, however, and Eve was often haunted by a deep sadness. It was not until a priest invited her to attend Mass in her early fifties that she began to discover that she was loved by the heavenly Father. Returning to the sacraments, she found this love was embracing her from within, like a light piercing through the shadow of her past sorrows. Eve could see that throughout her whole life, God had been pursuing her and teaching her that evil does not have the last word.

Eve accepted the physical and emotional suffering that she would experience in the later years of her life, saying, "Everything which happens to us has been foreseen from all eternity for the glory of God and our own greater good."[2] Christ was changing her history from

---

[1] Charlotte Kelly, *A Saint of the Stage: Eve Lavalliere* (Melbourne: Advocate Press, 1938), http://todayscatholicworld.com/Eve-Lavalliere-A-Saint-of-the-Stage-Imp-1936.pdf.

[2] Ann Ball, "Eve Lavalliere (1866–1929)," *Modern Saints: Their Lives and Faces*, bk. 2 (Gastonia, NC: TAN Books, 1991), see chap. 37.

anger to joy. Upon seeing an acquaintance from her acting days, she said, "When people mention me to you, make it quite clear to them, all those who know me, that you have seen the happiest, indeed, the most perfectly happy of women."[3] This love was the "sort of thing" she was made for.

Trust is the expectation of God's goodness to pervade my present, no matter what is contained in my past. Have I given up believing that God intends to share Himself with me *today*? Without the lens of an eternal love, suffering and death appear to be the worst, irreparable evils. If we live only for this passing world, and thus feel the losses of the past outside of their proper perspective, we can easily find our life flavored with deepening bitterness and blame.

Christ invites us to look up and believe the sun shines beyond the stormy clouds instead of freezing ourselves and others in the past. This doesn't mean, however, that we can dismiss our past. But if we live out of the wounds of our past, it holds us back from living and loving in our day-to-day life *now*. And our present moment will then become another regret. Eve could have lived from that dark moment; all the trauma of her childhood could have caused her to forever reject God. Instead, the Lord's plan placed her on the path of nonbelievers, for whom she would then intercede, to find the Light of Life.

[3] Ball, "Eve Lavalliere."

JESUS, I TRUST IN YOU

Coming through the locked doors of the upper room where His disciples were gathered on the evening of Easter Sunday, Jesus says, "Peace be with you" (John 20:19). The apostles were weighed down with the shame of abandoning Him in His Passion and death. Yet as Jesus said these words, He pointed to His wounds, now radiant with light. It was a newness of life that was victorious over all sin and death. His wounds silently spoke the utter reconciliation now between them: *Peace be with you.*

Jesus was keenly aware of the sufferings He had just undergone, and of the fears that gripped the apostles. He wanted for them the same glory the Father had manifested in Him through those very pains. Expressing the word of peace a second time, He stresses that He truly harbors no ill will against the apostles, or any of us. In this moment of forgiveness and restoration, Jesus chooses not only to bring healing to the apostles' burdened hearts but to share with them the authority to do likewise (John 20:21–23).

As Jesus stood among His apostles that night, He stands among us now. He is the only one who is fully aware of what our past contains, and He does not want to erase it. The *full* story of our past is only revealed when imbued with His mercy, and this is what makes the very things that are most difficult in our history have tremendous value. Jesus is the living embodiment of this: coming before the apostles, His resurrected body brightly bore the scars of His death. He shows us that the way to new life is through trusting His unconditional and victorious love—both in the forgiveness of our sins and in allowing us to see our past in the perspective of His eternal plan. Everything we've experienced, seen in the light of God's mercy, can truly make us rejoice in the glory of God.

Earlier in His ministry, Jesus referred to this as He quoted the psalms: "The very stone which the builders rejected has become the cornerstone" (Matt 21:42; Ps 118:22). We see Jesus as that stone, rejected and killed by His people, but now He is the firm foundation upon which our entire lives are securely built.

INVITATION

- Through revealing His presence with us in our past, we come to know and believe in God's infinite mercy. If I follow Jesus, the road always leads to mercy. If I have lost trust in God because of something in the past, am I willing to ask the Lord to show me the meaning of those experiences or relationships? Maybe you have assigned a meaning to a painful memory, but it might not be correct. For example, you may think that a relationship did not work out because you did not deserve it, rather than because God wanted something more for you. He may not answer everything immediately, but He desires to give His peace. Where do I want to believe and receive Jesus' words to me, "Peace be with you"?

- Resentment can occur when I experience being unjustly deprived of something I think I needed.

To remove this block in my relationship with the Lord, I can ask for the grace to freely give to God what I feel was taken from me. So, if my father neglected me when I was young and as a result, I had to grow up quickly, I can *give* God not only my desire for a father who was more present but also the years of childhood I felt I lost. What we give Him could be anything from my need to be needed, to my reputation, to my secure homelife, to my joy. This turns a place of sorrow into a place of love, helping us to acknowledge the grief and also accept the past. Trust extends backward: God is there too. For all the times we didn't give things over to the Lord in our past, He gives us new opportunities to now. Is there something I presently want to choose to give to Jesus?

- Be compassionate to those around you, as everyone is suffering something and we do not know what others are carrying. Consider doing some hidden kindness for another who is struggling, and pray that this time of suffering may be for them an encounter with God.

DAY 10

From restless self-seeking
in the present moment,
deliver me, Jesus.

How effortlessly we can be caught in a whirlwind of distractions, daydreams, or useless media! Learning how to best live in the present takes time, ironically. Looking back on our day, we can often wonder if we could have used the minutes and hours better. But this points to something deeper within every human heart. Whether it is subtle or clear, we have a tremendous thirst to be satisfied.

Without knowing what this longing is, and truly what our deepest needs are, we can struggle to focus our energy on what really matters. Instead, we veer onto the path toward frustration, boredom, and addiction. Self-seeking in the present moment can include empty entertainment, avoiding the difficult duties of our lives, distracting ourselves from pain, filling voids with noise, and placing my needs above those of others.

As much as the present moment carries, with its responsibilities and challenges, it also bears a perpetual summons to greatness—the call to love.

In the influential and wealthy circles of Turin, a boy named Pier Giorgio was born shortly after the turn of the twentieth century. From his youth, he was expected to follow in the footsteps of his father, who was the editor of the city's paper, *La Stampa*, and later a senator and an ambassador. Yet, to his father, Pier Giorgio was lacking the necessary gifts to excel in these fields; and his father was often brutal when expressing his disappointment to his son.

The glittering life of elite parties and important people meant little to Pier Giorgio, who, unlike his sister, rarely went to his father's gatherings. Instead he looked forward to bringing the leftover food and flowers to the slums of Turin. In addition to the many hours of study he would put in every day, he would also slip out of the house for daily Mass and evening adoration. His mother often accused him of wasting time, and tried to discourage him from his prayers and involvement with the needy. Although a failure in his family's eyes, Pier Giorgio continued to hold fast to what he knew was worth his time.

For him, each day was the opportunity to receive more of this God whom he loved and share Him with others. The mountains, which Pier Giorgio relished, were the familiar setting where he would arrange outings with friends to climb the rocky heights and pray together. Through him, others felt God's presence, as one of his friends attested, "Never before or since did nature itself seem to us as majestic and as pure as when we admired it together with him. . . . he always placed God as the tie that bound us together, and in God's name, he blessed our friendship, our joy, our every feeling, and every moment of life."[1]

---

[1] Maria Di Lorenzo, *Blessed Pier Giorgio Frassati: An Ordinary Christian* (Boston: Pauline Books & Media, 2003), 84.

Despite the hardness of his parents, Pier Giorgio was patient with his mother and ever respectful of his father. He was not afraid to be himself, playing practical jokes on his friends, singing off tune, and laughing loudly. Finding God in all things, he could receive the present moment for the gift it is—the meeting of God's life with ours.

Pier Giorgio died at only twenty-four years old, after contracting polio, but gathered at his funeral were thousands who had been touched by his life. In shock, his family began to understand who he was, and his father later admitted what had earlier fueled his animosity: "I saw in him all the things I wished I could be. . . . It seemed to me that that little bit of good there is in me was multiplied by the millions in Pier Giorgio."[2]

What about us? Have you experienced goodness that inspired you to spread it? Have you encountered a truth that helped reveal yourself to you? Or beauty that pierced your heart? Have you received a love that made the whole world seem new? Once we have, our time will never be the same. When God breaks in, we realize time is an eternal exchange. Every minute has infinite value.

While it is not bad to enjoy pastimes, when the focus is on *self* and my own gratification—even in harmless ways—it becomes exhausting. It makes us weary and restless, an indication that hopefully prompts us to keep searching for the something more our hearts long for. While God wants to satisfy us—and He alone does—it paradoxically happens as we turn our gaze not inward but outward.

Seeking our own fulfillment in the present moment

[2] Di Lorenzo, *Blessed Pier Giorgio Frassati*, 106.

hinders trust because it is based on the thinking that God will not satisfy us. With the eyes of trust, we come to see that the present moment contains within it the very light of heaven itself. Trust finds God in every moment.

JESUS, I TRUST IN YOU

"In those days Mary arose and went with haste into the hill country" (Luke 1:39). Mary had just conceived Christ within her and immediately sets out to help her cousin Elizabeth, who was miraculously pregnant after many childless years. Along the rigorous sojourn, she must have been continually lifted by the thought that the one who crafted the hillside was within her. How she must have praised Him for entering the creation she was beholding. Every ounce of her being was silently proclaiming what all creation longed for: God is here!

At a time when Mary could have easily stayed at home to prepare herself for Jesus' birth, surmising it was better to avoid a long and dangerous journey, she looked to serve another. The experience of the humility of God so recently impressed upon her—Him descending and becoming man for our sake—impelled her toward this generous self-forgetfulness.

When Mary entered the house and greeted her cousin, Elizabeth knew Mary was not alone, as Elizabeth's child "leaped in her womb" (Luke 1:41). She called Mary "the mother of my Lord" (v. 43) without any prior knowledge or visible proof. Upon hearing that Jesus' presence was recognized through her, Mary sang aloud the mystery: "My soul magnifies the Lord ... " (vv. 46–55). Her life radiated His. For thousands of years, prophets went to mountaintops to encounter God, but here in this lowly setting, the mountaintop had come to them. Through Mary they were given a stunning view of the summit.

We hear Jesus say in Matthew's Gospel, "You are the salt of the earth. . . . You are the light of the world. . . . Let your light so shine before men, that they may see your good works and give glory to your Father who is in heaven" (Matt 5:13–14, 16). Unlike Mary, who magnifies the Lord in a singular way, we may not be expecting these words or feel adequate to receive them. We don't know who we are to Him.

Yet, Jesus sees something significant in us that we often doubt and rarely live true to. He longs to light our hearts on fire with His presence. Every day we are called to carry Him within us and be His light in this world. And every day we are called to be salt for the world, bringing the flavor of His love to a culture bland from disillusionment. Spending my daily life on plans that are merely focused on myself is putting a bushel basket over what Jesus wants others to see and witness: His love radiating uniquely through you.

INVITATION

- Jesus is calling us higher, *verso l'alto*—to the heights—as Pier Giorgio Frassati would say! He asks us not to remain at the bottom; He wants to animate the entirety of our lives by sharing His life with us. We find God everywhere but in a special way in our neighbor. Looking outward, how can I serve the needs of others in my area?

• Am I in a battle against distractions, pulling me from things I need to do and stripping things of their joy? This may be acedia, which is a type of sloth that can pervade one's spiritual life. Setting guidelines for how much media time you have every day and when you choose to use it (not as a distraction, an escape, or to satisfy your curiosity instantly) will help immensely, as will cutting out the time-stealer and emotional boxing ring of daydreaming. Is there any distraction in my life that I need to cut out?

• How we spend our time shows us what's important to us. It is good to have some leisure in our lives and our hearts expand when exposed to beauty, truth, and goodness. Carve out time to spend receiving the gifts of nature, loved ones, books that inspire, and discussions that stir you toward holiness. Do I spend free time on things that glorify God (1 Cor 10:31)? Do I seek ways of building community?

Day 11

From disbelief in Your love and
presence, deliver me, Jesus.

After World War II, my mother's family was fortunate
to be reunited, as they, like many other families across
Europe, had been displaced and separated. But it would
not be for long. At age five, her father had the children and their mother pack their bags and move into a
small three-room apartment while he went to live with
another woman. The painful betrayal and the poverty
that it brought to their lives left my heartbroken mother
convinced God was far away. She did not hate God,
though. Rather, she was indifferent to Him, since she
felt He was indifferent to her, much like the statues of
Him she saw twice a year at the village church.

It's easy to follow her line of thinking, as many times
disbelieving in the Lord's presence, which is a loving
presence, comes from the false notion that the situations in our lives are too painful or sinful for Him to be
present. Or conversely, that life is too ordinary for God
to be intimately a part of it. We conclude that He has
walked out on us or is simply not interested in us.

At sixteen, my mom picked up a booklet with a
picture of Jesus on it, given to her by her mother, my
grandmother. She was less than inclined to look at
anything about God but had promised her mother she

would read it. Opening to a random page, my mom read the words of Jesus to a Polish sister, St. Faustina: "Let no soul fear to draw near to Me, even though its sins be as scarlet."[1] In a moment of sheer grace, she realized that someone was deeply interested in her and was loving her. The bitterness and unforgiveness began to melt. The truth of His loving presence throughout her life was so strongly impressed on her heart that, all of a sudden, it struck her as bizarre that she could be indifferent to Jesus, who was always thinking of her. For the next two hours, she knelt on her bedroom floor, weeping as she said over and over, "Jesus, from this day forward, I want to be your friend."

Based on her expectations of God and the absence of consoling feelings, she had assumed His distance. Yet it was not simply a feeling that convicted my mother of God's loving presence that night, but a grace He had been waiting to give at the first opening of her heart.

How do we recognize His presence? Would we have walked right past the Crucifixion, only sensing the evil present and not His love poured out there? Or passing through Nazareth, would we have not batted an eye in seeing the carpenter's family? For those who are open to truth—which is often far wider than my expectations— God reveals Himself.

Because He is God, there is a mysterious quality to Jesus' presence, which is often mistaken for a distance between Him and us. The times of greatest trial, when we least experience consoling feelings, are often when the Lord is very close. And then, seemingly without warning, we can be filled with a sense of His presence,

---

[1] Kowalska, *Diary of St. Faustina*, para. 699.

only for a time of seeming distance to follow, and so on. Consistency is a trait we associate with a trustworthy person, so the ebbs and flows in our *felt* relationship with God can be disorienting. Yet, God is always interested in each of us at every moment. He simply desires that we likewise are interested in *Him* and not just the way we feel—like all experiences of authentic love. Feelings are not bad, but as changing, they cannot be the lantern that guides us. We come to truly know God not through our feelings but in the faith that is forged in believing Him.

If we believe God does not care about us or has abandoned us, we lose the trust that He can reveal Himself to us in our present circumstances. And as the Lord pursues us, the distrustful heart will not invest in Him, thinking He will "leave" again. This holds us back, because as the Lord begins to heal us, we may not believe it, wondering if those graces will pass with our changing perceptions. Trust is staked on the fact that God is present no matter what we feel. In times when we do not feel His presence, we can remember that if God allows difficult suffering in our life, "He upholds it with an even greater grace, though we are not aware of it. One act of trust in such moments gives greater glory to God than whole hours passed in prayer filled with consolation."[2]

JESUS, I TRUST IN YOU

"I came that they may have life, and have it abundantly" (John 10:10). It is within the context of the passage about the good shepherd that Jesus shared this reason

---

[2] Kowalska, *Diary of St. Faustina*, para. 78.

for His presence among us. He is the Good Shepherd, who knows His sheep, and His sheep recognize His voice, which calls them to good pastures. Jesus acknowledged that others break into the sheepfold, thieves and robbers, with the intention to destroy, but "My sheep hear my voice . . . and they shall never perish, and no one shall snatch them out of my hand" (John 10:27–28).

The sheepfold of this life is shown as a vulnerable place. Thieves break in to destroy and hirelings flee when danger arrives, abandoning the sheep when the wolf comes. More than anyone, Jesus understands the anger that may result from this broken trust. It is a natural reaction and we can be angry at God, the person who hurt us, and ourselves for how we handled what was difficult.

Rather than inflicting punishment in the moment, or taking revenge (which is what justice seems to demand), Jesus goes beyond. Instead of an "eye for an eye," the Lord says, "Love your enemies and pray for those who persecute you" (Matt 5:44). He did not come to destroy, but proclaimed, "I lay down my life for my sheep" (John 10:15)

The Good Shepherd shows the sheep their worth. This is the one trait that Jesus points out for us to distinguish Him by. He has given His life in the fight for yours. Whatever harm we experience will not go unanswered. His mercy is always leading us to the ultimate pasture where there are no hirelings or thieves.

In the wake of choices, whether they be our own or those of others, that had destructive consequences, we may come to know more clearly the difference between the voice calling us to good pastures and the voice that leads to death. And it may be perhaps the place we come to know the value we have—listening to His voice, we come to know, "I know my own and my own know me" (John 10:14). This laying down of His life for me opens the gate to the eternal pastures where He "prepare[s] a table before me" (Ps 23:5). Despite feelings of abandonment in this life, Jesus' promise remains: "I am with you always" (Matt 28:20).

INVITATION

- Our feelings can confuse us, making "I don't feel love" synonymous with "I am not loved," and "I feel alone" with "I am alone." We have given feelings a false supremacy and must recognize that they are not a spiritual authority. At the same time, our feelings matter and are a great starting point for honest prayer. Suffering in silence, if motivated by a fear of vulnerability, can build animosity and irritation, while sharing it with the Lord first and foremost can dispel it. Where do I feel alone? Ask Jesus to show you how He is already present with you there.

- Even in our anger, Jesus shows us our worth. Jesus is not afraid of the quiet, passive anger, or even the blatant, aggressive anger, that can arise in the human heart. In fact, He is honored when we can come to Him in it, like a parent who treasures that their child trusts them enough to reveal what is causing them pain. In receiving it, He receives us and shows us that we do not have to live in anger. The very absorption of that anger by His love speaks of a real presence with us. Am I angry about anything? Can I look to Jesus as a safe harbor for acknowledging difficulties in my life?

- My mom came to know herself as the sheep rescued by the Lord. It was by hearing the truth of His words to her that she was able to recognize His voice speaking the truth of who she was, leading her to good pastures. Whether it is the death of a loved one, the misunderstanding of a boss, the ridicule of peers, or the absence of love from a parent, we have received hurts in the "sheepfold" of life that we did not ask for. Yet, do we recognize the voice of the Good Shepherd? Jesus wants to anoint us with oil, bind our wounds, and give us rest by receiving us in these places of pain that make us doubt His presence.

DAY 12

From the fear of being asked to give more than I have, deliver me, Jesus.

When St. Francis first heard the call to serve God in the poor, he took cloth from his father, who was a well-to-do merchant, sold it, and gave the money to the poor. The "Robin Hood" mentality suited the situation, as God appeared to be asking him something beyond his personal means. When Francis' father helped him to see that he was in fact stealing, Francis saw more clearly what God had intended. Having encountered Jesus in the poor, Francis set out to become poor himself, renouncing worldly riches and honors so as to imitate Christ. And it was only then, as a beggar, that he would receive another call from the Lord in prayer: "Repair My House, which is falling in ruins."[1] How can one man rebuild God's house, the Church, much less a poor man?

In his poverty, Francis had started to learn that it was less about what God expected of him and more of what he expected of God. Before the fuller meaning was made known to him, St. Francis did what he could

---

[1] Omer Englebert, *St. Francis of Assisi: A Biography* (Ann Arbor, MI: Servant Books, 1979), 33.

to follow that call. With donated stone and mortar, he repaired three churches in his hometown of Assisi. Without St. Francis intending it, followers arrived and numbered over three thousand a dozen years later. They went preaching the Gospel all over Italy and then beyond, living with the poor and giving all they had to the refuse of society.

St. Francis saw poverty as the pathway to God's plenty because it was fertile ground for living the trust Jesus likewise lived. So, opened by the meager means he had, St. Francis' trust in the Lord was more than enough to live the Lord's wild invitations to him, which stretched beyond him. Pope Innocent III, after seeing St. Francis upholding the pillars of the Church in a dream, approved his order. His order's widespread, tangible witness restored an authentic trust in the Gospel, repairing the crumbling faith of many hearts in the Church.

God will never ask us to give more than we have. Although the task He invites us to may exceed our capacities, the gift of our love and consent to Him is all He is looking for. In fact, because things don't seem to add up in our estimation, the gift of our trust in His power pleases Him greatly. Our trust in Him gives Him the freedom to multiply our small efforts, allowing God to pour His love through us.

The fear in this invitation is that we'll fall short and won't be enough. We can wonder if God is setting us up for failure. "He doesn't know me," or, "He's mistaken about me. I can't possibly do what He is asking." "Another child, now? Do I have it in me?" "Caring for my elderly parents?" "Breaking this addiction?" "Defending my faith at work?" . . . *I can't*. And there is some truth to that. On my own, I can't. But if the Lord is asking, then He wants to act in and through us—right here, in the midst of challenges and chaos. Trust allows the Lord to live a love within me that is beyond my capacity, to be in us what we cannot be on our own.

JESUS, I TRUST IN YOU

Walking the path to Calvary, Simon of Cyrene was enlisted to help Jesus carry His Cross (Mark 15:21). It was clear to the Roman soldiers that Jesus might not make it otherwise. Jesus seemed to be teetering on the very edge of what was possible.

As we pray the Stations of the Cross, we see Jesus fall not once or twice, but three times, even with Simon's help. Crushed and exhausted, He tasted the full gravity of weakness and broke through its limits. While every ounce of his body clamored, *I can't*, He chose to trust the strength of the Father's call to rise and get up again. The way chosen to save us was a path of trust in the face of seeming inability. To repair the distrust of sin, Jesus, in every step, was truly restoring trust in the Father.

After Jesus' Resurrection, He asked Peter, who had denied Him three times, "Peter, do you love me?" Following Peter's affirmative but mild response, Jesus entrusts to him the flock of the Church, and asks him again. (See John 21:15–16.) And then a third time, which grieved Peter (John 21:17). Peter did not feel confident in his ability to be faithful to Jesus, although he desired to be. Remembrance of his weakness may have still plagued him with the thought *I can't*.

Jesus was not only drawing out from Peter a proc-lamation to repent of his denials but was longing to show Peter who He really was. As his Savior, Jesus had the trust Peter was lacking. In accepting the feeble yet sincere love of Peter, Jesus was saying, *I know you, and I want you to know Me. I want you to believe that trusting in My love more than in your own strength shows Me that you know Me.* Jesus has already carried our crosses and won that ability to trust for us, especially when it seems like God is asking more than we think we have. How God honors us by bringing the nobility of His love to the depths of our frailty!

INVITATION

- Whatever God is asking, He will provide for all we lack. A couple I know was asked if they wanted to adopt the preemie baby boy they had been fos-tering. With so many unknowns about what his needs would be in the future, they did not know how to discern what was best. Yet, one question became paramount: Is God asking this of us? If He is, then He will supply what is needed. When making decisions, do I look at what I have or what God is asking?

- Just as Francis felt small in the face of what God was asking, we too can feel overwhelmed by what God is inviting us to. This is the very place He wants to restore trust in our hearts. Praying for the gift of Jesus' trust, already claimed by Him for us, we realize our seeming incapacity no longer impedes the gift of ourselves. Where do I feel like God is asking something more than I think I have?

- Gratitude increases our trust. Can we recount with gratitude times that we have seen Him provide, multiplying our efforts? Let your gratitude rouse you to pray for more than you think is possible, as St. Francis did: *Most High, glorious God, enlighten the darkness of my heart and give me true faith, certain hope, and perfect charity, sense, and knowledge, Lord, that I may carry out Your holy and true command.*

DAY 13

<hr />

From the belief that my life has no meaning or worth, deliver me, Jesus.

Walter Ciszek, a rough kid from Shenandoah, Pennsylvania, who had a propensity for mischief, surprised his family in entering the seminary. His stubbornness, once used in defiance of authority, was now harnessed toward becoming a saint—in his own image of what it meant to be holy. He would be no ordinary priest, however, and pushed himself in seminary to make rigorous fasts and keep a tight schedule.

Aiming for the most radical mission of bringing Christ to others, he volunteered to become an undercover priest in the Soviet Union. It was a risky endeavor, and within two years of his arrival he was arrested. Being drugged into signing a declaration that he was a Vatican spy with political aims, Fr. Walter spent a total of twenty-three years in prison and labor camps in Siberia. To be looked at as a spy was to be constantly distrusted. Being treated so severely, and being very limited in sharing the sacraments he had worked so hard to bring to these people, he battled feeling unnecessary and questioned his worth.

The hinge for his sanity was the invitation to accept

his situation as God's will in total trust and to thus offer God his life, precisely in his present circumstance. Of this Fr. Ciszek writes, "He was asking a complete gift of self, nothing held back. . . . Like the eternity between anxiety and belief when a child first lets go of all support—only to find that the water truly holds him up and he can float motionless, and totally relaxed."[1] It was not intuitive in these disparaging circumstances, but Fr. Ciszek was convinced that if God had offered His life for him, there was great meaning in his life. He would live that truth in trust by daily offering his life back to God.

This act of love, which is an act of trust, grounded him in his priceless dignity, allowing him to thrive in the most grueling of situations. Even giving our misery to God is a gift that He yearns to receive.

Wherever we find ourselves, we are infinitely loved by God. And wherever we find ourselves, love is possible. God's love is our worth, as we have been bought "with the precious blood of Christ" (1 Pet 1:19). This love that defines us cannot be taken from us. A difficult break-up, severe health problems, job loss, betrayals, "tribulation, or distress, or persecution, or famine, or nakedness, or peril, or sword . . . neither death, nor life, nor angels, nor principalities, nor things present, nor things to come, nor powers, nor height, nor depth, nor anything else in all creation, will be able to separate us from the love of God in Christ Jesus our Lord" (Rom 8:35, 38–39).

We may never end up in a prison, but the lies of the culture can push us into believing we are trapped,

---

[1] Walter J. Ciszek, *He Leadeth Me: An Extraordinary Testament of Faith* (Garden City, NY: Doubleday, 1973), 88–89.

without hope or a purpose. Disoriented by sin and suffering, and having our trust broken, we can think we are useless to society, like a burden to be forgotten. When we live in these horrendous conditions, Jesus' voice tells us that there are no locks on the doors of our inner prison. Yet He does not force us to believe Him. "Behold, I stand at the door and knock; if any one hears my voice and opens the door, I will come in" (Rev 3:20).

Fr. Ciszek discovered that by giving your life away for another, you actually receive it as a new and unrepeatable gift. Only in God's eyes do we see the truth that no one can love with *my* heart, that my love is utterly unique. Fr. Ciszek believed his survival and eventual release back to the United States was to witness the faithfulness of God to each person, exhorting them to be anchored in the ultimate reality of their lives. Trust receives the truth of my inestimable worth in God's eyes.

JESUS, I TRUST IN YOU

There is a Gospel passage that tells of a man who urgently came to Jesus, pleading to save his twelve-year-old daughter's life—she was "at the point of death" (Mark 5:23). On His way to heal her, Jesus is unexpectedly stopped. A woman who had been hemorrhaging for twelve years reached out to touch His garments, in hopes that He would cure her. In that culture, someone who is bleeding is untouchable. This woman must have been struggling deeply, thinking, "I am unwanted, undesirable, unattractive, and worthless." Even though she "had spent all that she had" on remedies that never worked, she believed a mere touch of Jesus' hem would heal her (vv. 25–28). And she was right.

In the midst of a full crowd, Jesus felt this healing power released from Him and asked aloud, "Who touched my garments?" (Mark 5:30). Many had physically touched Him as He walked by, but who was the one who had found this complete access to His heart? Because she was considered unclean, she confessed in fear what she had done. Jesus was not upset, however, but was impressed by her faith.

She, who thought her life and love was useless, had moved the heart of God Himself. Although she was avoided by others, Jesus had received her love and willingly delayed His urgent mission because He wanted her to know how powerful it was.

It was just then that Jesus heard that the little girl who was sick had died. Still fresh with the offering of the hemorrhaging woman's faith, Jesus looked to the father of the girl and said, "Do not fear, only believe" (Mark 5:36). Upon taking this girl's hand, Jesus called to her, "Little girl, I say to you, arise" (v. 41).

This is a striking image. It is as if the Lord wanted to show with these juxtaposed stories that this woman who had been bleeding for twelve years felt like the child inside of her was dying. The child who dreamed of love, and who was filled with hope for her future, was at the point of death. Ready to give up on herself, she received the grace to believe Jesus had not—and it changed everything for her. Giving the gift of her trust to Jesus—which is an expression of love—wholly revived her.

At the end of every day when I pray Night Prayer

with my Sisters, the words "Into Your hands, O Lord, I commend my spirit" are chanted. They are the words of Jesus, who, at the point of death, made the final offering of His life to the Father (Luke 23:46). In what seemed like a useless, degrading death, "Christ saved the world when He was hanging helplessly on the Cross."[2] Jesus trusted in the love of the Father and offered His own life in faith. What possibly can stand against this power?

INVITATION

- We each have standards for determining self-worth, and they profoundly affect how we view our life. Take some time in prayer to ask the Lord to reveal to you "What are my measures for self-worth?" and "How do I measure my worth?" He may illuminate the ways you look to others for self-worth, or have thought of yourself as useless or unnecessary after your trust was broken, or how your day-to-day life seems useless. Are my standards for the value of my life the same as the Lord's?

- Many of us in our culture know the experience of being at the point of death interiorly. We too may have spent all we have, only to still battle the lies against our life. The gift of my love combats the deception that my life is not valued or precious, whether it be a small act of love for that person in your family that you feel a bit distant from, doing

2 John Cardinal O'Connor, "Give God Permission," *Catholic New York*, May 25, 1995.

the task at work that no one wants to do, or volunteering some of your time. Realizing that your love is unique and that no one can love with your heart, is there a place God is inviting you to share your love?

• Offering our love to God with trust is powerful. Wherever I am in my relationship with the Lord, can I pause at least once a day to make a small offering of my life to God, in my own words? It can be as simple as saying, "Jesus, I give You my life," or, "Jesus, I trust You with my life," or, "Father, into Your hands I commend my spirit." I've made it a habit to offer my life to God every time I bow my head in saying the Glory Be prayer, using something that is already a part of my day to let His power course through me.

DAY 14

———◦•◦———

From the fear of what love demands, deliver me, Jesus.

When someone begins to fall in love, the other person pierces through to a deep place in the heart, and in the excitement that lifts them, their existence no longer seems ordinary. Yet the vulnerability of love, as beautiful as it is, can scare us. It is as if the human heart knows "I will lose myself in this love; it's larger than me." As much as we want it, we know, "To love is enormously demanding."[1]

So much in our modern mindset follows the axiom "How can I get the most for putting in the least?" And it trickles down into so many of our thoughts. How can I enjoy the most amount of flavor with the least amount of weight gain? How can I have the best prayer life with the least amount of effort? How can I get to heaven with the least amount of commitment? And how can I be happily in love with the least amount of sacrifice?

We've tried to convince ourselves that this mentality is for our benefit, and so we continue to calculate our happiness through the balance of what we get versus what we give. After all, a lot of people enjoy diet soda, some people win the lottery every year, and the good

---

[1] John Cardinal O'Connor, "Introduction Conference," Sisters of Life 3rd discernment retreat, Yonkers, NY, December 31, 1992.

thief was promised paradise at the moment of his death. It may not sound like a big deal to ask what's in it for me, but it has become the lens through which we see marriage, children, work ethics, discerning a vocation, ourselves, and even God. Yet this is the slippery slope of distrust, which is not truly open to living real love for fear it will cost me more than I want to invest. What's the alternative?

As a young soldier recovering from a battle injury on his leg in 1521, St. Ignatius of Loyola spent long hours dreaming about a noble woman he was attracted to and what he would do to gain her affection. To further pass the time, he was given a book on the lives of the saints and a book on the life of Christ, which began to stir his heart with desires to fight for the kingdom of God. Considering the path of worldly honors and glory versus imitating the saints, he learned how to distinguish the movements of his heart and how God was drawing him to a life of virtue, which he would outline in his writings on the discernment of spirits.

Ignatius came to see the compelling force of our desires, the greatest being love. In the very slight chance that Ignatius would win this woman's heart as a knight in court, he had his leg reset and sawed twice without anesthesia, purely to avoid a limp and unsightly bulge. Yet, as much as he desired the love of this woman, he eventually found himself even more impelled to give up these pursuits out of love for Christ. As he deepened in his awareness of God's love for him through repentance and prayer, Ignatius took notes on his interior experiences.

From these notes, Ignatius developed a retreat framework that culminates in praying to receive a greater love for the Lord. St. Ignatius thus provided a prayer in response to this love of God, called the *Suscipe*. In Latin, *suscipe* means "receive," and it is a prayer asking God to receive all of me. It ends with "Grant me only to love you, give me this grace. This, truly, is enough for me."[2] Here, St. Ignatius asks for more love of God (rather than simply knowing His love for us), because the more love of God we receive, the more will our hearts be given generously, without counting the cost and without fearing demands. The openness to this love is trust, which helps us to see a value beyond the apparent sacrifices. Trust allows the heart to be compelled by love.

JESUS, I TRUST IN YOU

As Jesus set out on a journey, we hear of an encounter with a rich young man who asked Jesus what he must do to inherit eternal life (see Mark 10:17–22). After Jesus asks him to follow the commandments, this man, earnestly kneeling before Jesus, professes that he had been obeying them for years. Before Jesus answers further, we hear, "And Jesus looking upon him loved him" (v. 21). It must have been such a strong gaze of love that even those standing by noticed it.

Jesus then said, "You lack one thing," and told him to sell his possessions, give to the poor so as to store

[2] For more information on the *Suscipe* (and the full prayer), see David Coffey, "The Ignatian *Suscipe* Prayer: Its Text and Meaning," *Journal of Jesuit Studies* 5, no. 4 (November 15, 2018): 511–529, https://brill.com/view/journals/jjs/5/4/article-p511_511.xml?language=en.

up treasure in heaven, and follow Him (Mark 10:21). At this, the man became sad and walked away, possibly never raising his eyes to see Jesus' look. The young man must have really been asking, "How can I gain heaven without letting go of earth?" He wanted to inherit eternal life, yet the scale of what was worthwhile tipped for him and he only saw the price. Jesus saw that this man's wealth was tied to his self-image. In His mercy, Jesus was offering Himself as the true wealth, with a demand that would free him from hiding behind what he had placed his trust in.

It *does* cost us to follow Jesus and to be with Him forever. He is not afraid to ask us to make a sacrifice in His name, because the truth is that we gain far more than we give. Trust helps us set out on the journey with Jesus without calculating what is in it for me, but out of love of Him. We may not be asked to sell all that we have to give to the poor, but Jesus asks each one of us to prefer Him to riches and our own comfort. Thus the precious trust in our hearts will not be given to things that pass away but to Him.

As the young man walked away, Jesus said to the disciples, "Children, how hard it is for those who trust in riches to enter the kingdom of God!" (Mark 10:24). These possessions and pleasures may not be bad, but they often put Jesus on the periphery of our hearts. He asks us to give away that which will make room for Him to share life together with us. The generosity of our response to Him will never be regretted. Rather, we will only stand in thanksgiving for the freeing nature of His invitations of love to us.

INVITATION

- When we encounter the demands of love, the Lord intends a gift for us, in the very cost. If we are struggling with chastity, is He inviting us to a deeper love? When asked to let go of an attachment or doing something my way, is He paving a path for greater freedom? Take a moment to consider: Is there a place in my heart that I am resisting the requirements of love? We can pray with St. Ignatius for more love of God—not only to see His loving look upon me but, for His sake, to respond without fear of what the road ahead entails.

- It can be tempting to count the cost, but as soon as we begin calculating, the doors of our hearts start shutting in self-protection. Has this mentality of measuring what I give versus what I get shaped my view of the world? It can cause us to seek pleasure and comfort and to avoid taking due responsibility because of the cost—parents who shrink from proper discipline, fair-weather friends, opting to use contraception, or choosing to remain ignorant about the teachings of the Church.

- Any serious Christian can say that at times our bodies hate the journey, just like any serious athlete would say. Sacrifice is not a way of rejecting ourselves nor a way to better ourselves. Rather, it is an expression of giving ourselves in love for another. We should be able to devote a fraction of what we do to stay in shape, or to get rave reviews at work, to our relationship with God. Every day we can offer some bodily mortification not for myself but for love of Him. Whether that is getting up early in the morning to pray, going without something I enjoy eating, or lowering the knob on our hot shower, we are making greater room for Jesus to be the true wealth in our hearts.

DAY 15

From discouragement,
deliver me, Jesus.

There is a little phrase in Matthew's Gospel right after Peter has denied Christ multiple times: "Peter remembered" (Matt 26:75). It hits Peter that Jesus told him this would happen. *Peter remembered.* What a moment! In the sorrow and pain of Peter's heart, he would have been tempted to shut his heart in despair, but instead he left it cracked open and was flooded with a deep consolation. Jesus knew and still called him friend. Nothing is hidden from Him and He still loves us. This assurance, once tasted, is hard to shake.

How many times we can walk into a church or begin to pray, and our downfalls, failures, and sins flash in front of the eyes of our soul, making us think they're all God sees when He looks at us. When we ask Him, however, He never fails to show us differently.

Discouragement happens because we want to be in a better place than we find ourselves, and while that sounds noble, it stems from what we all battle: pride. Humble people are not surprised or deterred by their weaknesses, because they know they are but limited creatures before God. They also know that God knows and loves them all the while. They live in the confidence that Jesus saves.

Therefore, discouragement is not trusting that Jesus is who He is, my Savior. Instead, the discouraged heart proclaims that it is its own savior. Understandably, in this perspective we become quite deflated because we're significantly underqualified.

We typically become discouraged about ourselves or about the world around us. In the first case, I become more aware that in the midst of my daily life, my will to choose what is good is weak. We can only agree with St. Paul: "For I do not do the good I want, but the evil I do not want is what I do" (Rom 7:19). We simply can't get it together and "fix" ourselves. And in the second case, I can feel that I am a victim of circumstances that seem oppressive.

When we experience discouragement because of our sins, we need to reconsider temptations from the right perspective. No one spends their energy on ripping apart what is already destroyed. The evil one wants to ruin what is *good*. That's his entire plan. So I experience temptations not because I'm bad, but because at the core of my being, I am good. Far from being exempt from temptation, the great saints suffered tremendous temptations but did not consent to them. They saw that there was something precious offered to us in each temptation. Resisting temptations is the *purest* way to love the Lord. To choose God there, where I feel no benefit for myself at that moment, and to do it for Him alone is real love. He is honored to be loved by us in that occasion.

While we are discouraged about the world around us or those in our lives, we fail to trust that God is laboring to love there. No situation is without hope. If we are moved to sorrow or anger, God may be awakening in us, through that, a deeper love for others. How many charitable foundations emerge from a suffering that now expresses itself in love? When frustrated with a lack of tangible results or appreciation, we can look to the simple advice of St. John of the Cross, who said, "Where there is no love, put love, and you will draw out love."[1] Every time we are tempted to be discouraged, doing a simple act of love for another immediately fights the lie that we are at a dead end.

JESUS, I TRUST IN YOU

Jesus was led by the Spirit into the wilderness (Matt 4:1; Luke 4:1–2). This was immediately following Jesus' baptism, where the voice of the Father proclaimed, "This is my beloved Son" (Matt 3:17). It was intended that the revealing of Jesus' identity as "Son" be linked together with His time in the desert. Many Church Fathers point out that Jesus' temptations in the desert all attack who He is as Son.[2] The first two temptations are phrased, "If you are the Son of God," to imply that because Jesus is experiencing these difficult things, He surely does not have a Father who cares about Him. *This* is the wilderness of the human heart, which Jesus enters for us. These are our temptations that He experiences. We are fragile and needy, doubting who we are in the hour we most need to stand in that truth. Here, in

---

[1] St. John of the Cross, *The Collected Works of St. John of the Cross*, trans. Kieran Kavanaugh and Otilio Rodriguez, rev. ed. (Washington, DC: ICS Publications, 1991), 760.

[2] For example, see St. Irenaeus, *Against Heresies* IV.6.6.

this rocky, arid place, Jesus claims who He is and who the Father is.

And He wins the strength for us to do the same.

Throughout the course of His public ministry, the temptation to be discouraged could have loomed overhead for Jesus, as He saw people attack Him and reject His love. Even in this assault on His sonship, nothing could come up against or change His beloved identity as Son of the Father. And nothing changes *who* we are, made in His image and invited into His life forever. What Jesus experienced in temptations is also what He desires for us during temptations: a turning to the Father, for which we always receive a blessing. He asks us to trust that "he who began a good work in you will bring it to completion" (Phil 1:6).

INVITATION

- As the Spirit allows, we experience temptations, but God offers us the opportunity to claim who we are as His son or daughter by rejecting lies about our worth. Where is the wilderness of my own heart, where I live thinking I have no Father? Do I have a plan for when discouraging thoughts come my way, either in the midst of temptations or afterward, to reject those lies? A simple phrase, such as "I do not consent," stops these thoughts from coming into our hearts. St. John Vianney said, "He who, when tempted, makes the Sign of the Cross with devotion, makes Hell tremble and Heaven rejoice."[3] You can also keep some holy water in your house to bless your home and loved ones.

- *Peter remembered.* In times of discouragement or failure, we can feel sad either because we've hurt Jesus or because our pride was hurt. Is there a moment that you have experienced one of these? Both can be a springboard for a deepened relationship with Jesus. Realizing we may have pained Jesus, who has never stopped loving us, we can become personally aware of the profundity of His love. And, in being humbled in our estimation of ourselves, we can grow by placing our confidence in His mercy, and not leaning on our pride, the source of discouragement. But we all have a choice to make in these moments: do we want to remain open to love?

- Discouragement tempts us to not try. Ask for the grace of the strengthening of my will in choosing what is good in my daily life and practice it in little ways. For example, setting a time to go to bed and a time to rise, and sticking to it; or becoming aware of near occasions of sin and making resolutions to avoid them.

[3] St. John Vianney, *Thoughts of the Curé D'Ars* (Rockford, IL: TAN Books, 1984), 26.

DAY 16

—◦•◦—

That You are continually holding me, sustaining me, loving me, Jesus, I trust in You.

How is it that the force of gravity is pulling matter together, while at the same time energy is causing the universe to expand . . . yet all is held in the proper balance? Stars and galaxies can form and develop, but the universe is protected from collapsing in on itself. Even on a smaller scale, the ornate designs on seahorses, the jagged structure of lightning, and the self-replicating patterns in everyday frost are beautifully ordered. Things seemingly un-orchestrated are gems of precision.

If this is true on the level of a fern leaf and the tip of a snowflake, what about for us? We have a capacity that science cannot explain, one that extends beyond our cellular function with the ability to wonder at the "whys" of life. We're in the realm of someone who left His imprint everywhere. The more we know Him, the easier it is to recognize that a flood of thoughtfulness envelopes me at every moment, healthy or sick, for I *am* a living, breathing masterpiece of God.

We are not mass produced but are crafted one by one. Our lip prints and toe prints, ear shapes and tongues, are totally unique, yet each of us senses our individuality beyond the anatomical. As hard as we try, we are unable to experience life, or any single event, exactly as another does, or to completely feel what another feels, or share everything we think. We connect with others, but our souls are ever distinct. Does anyone know the whole of me? Can anyone ever hold the fullness of who I am? The psalmist writes, "Where shall I go from your Spirit? Or where shall I flee from your presence? If I ascend to heaven, you are there! If I make my bed in Sheol, you are there! If I take the wings of the morning and dwell in the uttermost parts of the sea, even there your hand shall lead me. . . . even the darkness is not dark to you, the night is bright as the day; for darkness is as light with you" (Ps 139:7–10, 12).

Although he had been fairly pious as a child growing up in a Jewish family, Roy lost his belief in God when he went off to university to study science. A few years later, despite the worldly success of being a professor at Harvard Business School, he despaired because, with no God, there still was no real meaning or purpose to life. In this despondency, he was walking early one morning alone in a nature preserve on Cape Cod, having long since given up any hope in the existence of God, when he found himself suddenly very immediately aware of God's presence, and in an intimate state of communication with Him. Roy saw his life as though he had died and was looking over his life in the presence of God after death. He saw how deeply he would regret "all of the time and energy which I had wasted worrying about not being loved, when every moment of my existence I was held in the sea of God's unimaginably great love."[1] Roy saw that not only did God know him by name, but He had watched over him every moment since conception and had arranged absolutely everything that had ever happened to him. God cared so deeply about him that, in a very real way, everything that made Roy happy made Him happy, and everything that made Roy sad made Him sad, as though Roy was the only person God had ever created. Coming into this realization of God's very personal love for him resulted in a total redirection of his life. He now knew that the purpose of his life was to worship and serve this God. Once he realized that the Catholic Church was the truest way to do this, he dedicated his life to sharing the truths of the faith as a speaker and an author. The despair he had suffered prior to his rediscovery of God had been the echo of God in his heart calling him home.[2]

Trust has the courage to follow the heart's own depths, knowing God is waiting there.

JESUS, I TRUST IN YOU

Jesus' love for each person is unique. He healed individuals, called His disciples by name, and spent time listening to the plight of person after person. His encounter with the woman at the well (John 4:1–42)

---

[1] Roy Schoeman, *Salvation Is from the Jews* (San Francisco: Ignatius Press, 2003), 359.

[2] Roy's conversion story is taken from Roy Schoeman, "Roy Schoeman's Conversion Story," *Christ to the World* (July–August 2002): 253–260, https://www.catholiceducation.org/en/faith-and-character/faith-and-character/roy-schoeman-s-conversion-story.html.

offers us a glimpse of how tailored His heart is to each of us. Although she likely is not aware of her search for God at the moment, Jesus initiates the conversation by asking her for a drink. Shocked that He would be interested in associating with her, for she was a Samaritan woman, she is further surprised by His offer to her, "If you knew the gift of God, and who it is that is saying to you, 'Give me a drink,' you would have asked him and he would have given you living water" (John 4:10), referring to the grace of Baptism and the gift of the Holy Spirit. She responds as we often do. Doubting the Lord's capacity to really meet us in the depths, she says that the cistern is deep and He has nothing to lower into it. However, she confesses that she desires this living water to satiate her thirst and so that she does not have to keep coming back to the well.

Little does she know that Jesus is already in the depths of her heart's cistern. The conversation continues as He reveals to her the number of false lovers she has had, which convinces her He is at least some type of prophet, able to read her soul. Jesus indeed is in this cavernous place of her longing, of her search for love that not one of these "husbands" could satisfy. Realizing that her soul is exposed to Him, with its extensive thirst to be known and loved, why did she not excuse herself and walk away at that point, feeling judged? Afterward she even proclaimed publicly, with joy, that someone had told her all she had done. This was the content of her message and what brought all the people of her town out to see Jesus (John 4:29–30). She wasn't slighted; rather, this experience of being deeply known prompted her to ask Jesus about where one should worship God.

This inner place of thirst she has now accessed is where the longing to worship God is.

Knowing that she is not a Jew like Jesus is, she might have, for the first time, been pained by the sharp thought that she was excluded from what could satisfy her. Jesus spoke right to this deep place of her longing, saying that although salvation is from the Jews, true worship is not reserved for them alone. True worship is found in Jesus, who is the Truth, revealed by the Spirit. Trusting His love, through which she knows she is known and now is invited to belong, she can rest in this right worship of the one who alone holds all of her.

INVITATION

- There is a space within where no one but God has access. It is here I encounter Him, who knows the ways I have looked for love. The regrets, heartaches, betrayals, and humiliations, as well as the joys and desires. Experiencing this personal knowledge opens our hearts in trust to worship the one who continues to love us as He holds the whole of our lives. When I don't feel understood or supported, can I take a few minutes to share that with Christ, making this an opportunity for belonging rather than isolation? "You know that the foundation of the world is love, so that even when no human being can or will help you, you may go on, trusting in the One who loves you."[3]

---

[3] Joseph Ratzinger, "The Lord's Second Temptation," in *Jesus of Nazareth: From the Baptism in the Jordan to the Transfiguration* (San Francisco: Doubleday, 2007), 38.

- Whether we realize it or not, we worship whomever we look at to fill that deep space within—maybe another, myself, an ideology, or God. Yet God alone is deserving of our worship, as our Creator. He who holds us in existence shows us that the very depth of our hearts points us to loving an eternal, personal God. Worshipping God is an expression of trust, a response to His continual attentiveness to me in sustaining my life. When I go to Mass, can I pray by consciously opening my heart to receive God and to give my love to God, through this communal and individual worship of Him?

- We can connect with friends or catch up with a spouse about our day, and still feel unmet. In this, God is inviting us to become aware of the sacredness of this space and thus reverence it not only in our own heart but in those around us. Am I expecting my friends to fill me or trying to consume my spouse? Alternatively, we'll never be able to meet the infinite needs of another person; so, likewise, we can begin to recognize when to point them toward the Lord, who is awaiting a more personal encounter with them.

DAY 17

That Your love goes deeper than my sins and failings and transforms me, Jesus, I trust in You.

"I have seen the Lord" were Mary Magdalene's words announcing that Jesus had risen from the dead that first Easter morning (John 20:18). And these are the same words expressed in the lives of so many who have been wondrously changed. For each of us there is no better way to describe the effect of encountering a God who has conquered sin. As an expression of the Resurrection, the transformation to holiness baffles the world as it changes the world.

In hearing the stories of thousands of people over the years, either in the midst of my travels as a sister or in speaking over the phone or on retreats, the doubt that God's love is truly deeper and transformative comes up the most. Whether explicitly acknowledged or not, the struggle to believe this underlies the stagnancy of many hearts in the spiritual life.

It may be fairly easy to see some progress as we turn our hearts initially to the Lord, but often as we dive deeper into our faith journey and still struggle, we lower our expectations of God. "This is my cross" is used to explain stubborn habits—be it overeating, critical thoughts, unforgiveness, or lust—as if we are heroic in making a lifetime commitment to them. However, God does not desire our slavery. "For freedom Christ has set us free" (Gal 5:1). While we experience these weaknesses as a cross, since they are a burden to us, the Cross of Christ is something that brings freedom, not chains. Temptations and trials will continue, which St. Paul refers to as a "thorn . . . in the flesh" (2 Cor 12:7), but to consent to the ways they hold us back from real love is never His invitation. God wants abundantly more for us!

When the young St. Edmund Campion, one of England's finest orators, was pressured to compromise his faith, he fled in fear. Yet not only did he return to his country, he went back knowing he would be a hunted man, and thus inspired courage in the hearts of many before giving his life for his Catholic beliefs. St. Teresa of Avila, who was lax for the first twenty years of her religious life and even stopped praying, would later go beyond the resolution to just live faithfully. She went on to become a doctor of the Church for her insights on the most sublime heights of prayer. Both of them, in the midst of recognizing their own shortcomings, saw that the Lord had never compromised in loving them. Humbled by this reality, they embraced a new life that was truer to their hearts, for fear was not true to St. Edmund nor laxity to St. Teresa.

Because we have been created in the image and likeness of God, we were made for greatness. Yet we get attacked in the very place God wants to shine forth brilliantly. Sin is the epitome of inauthenticity. Pride, which is at the root of so many vices, tries to steal what does not belong to us. It breathes falsehood, leaving the authentic me obstructed from view and unknown. Because of this, as our hearts are transformed, it's an adjustment to allow the Lord to reveal to us who we really are.

I remember the day I got my braces off after two long teenage years. At first I didn't like my un-studded smile simply because I felt like it didn't look like me! It was actually more "me" than the metal-planked version, but I had gotten so used to what braces added to my appearance. If this is true on an external level, give yourself time when trying to get used to being who God created you to be, especially when there is habitual sin attached. We get accustomed to being inauthentic, and therefore it feels normal for us. So when our anger gets out of control or we choose to dwell on another's faults, we can easily think, "Well, that's just who I am." But no, it's not.

Transformation happens as we trust that His love is deeper than anything that besets us. St. John Paul II wrote that the one who receives mercy, this uncondi-tional love of God toward us in our misery, "does not feel humiliated, but rather found again and 'restored to value.'"[1] In response, we are drawn to spend time with Him in silent prayer, where God Himself will pursue amazing feats of transformation within our souls. Trust gives God permission to re-create us.

---

[1] John Paul II, Encyclical Letter on the Mercy of God *Dives in Miser-icordia* (November 30, 1980), §6.

JESUS, I TRUST IN YOU

Jesus is refreshingly authentic. And no one wants more for us than Jesus. He wants to give us new life. In Him, the prophets are fulfilled: "A new heart I will give you, and a new spirit I will put within you; and I will take out of your flesh the heart of stone and give you a heart of flesh" (Ezek 36:26). Jesus restored our relationship with the Father, dying our death for us that we may be "partakers of the divine nature" (2 Pet 1:4). He wants to heal us, not merely to be freed from eternal death, but to have everlasting life.

From Mary Magdalene, Jesus cast out seven demons (Luke 8:2; Mark 16:9), revealing that she was entrenched in a life of sin. He continued to call her to genuine discipleship by visiting her family home and instructing her in the good news of salvation. Jesus saw in her the one who would announce His Resurrection and began in her what would be the invitation for all Christians: the transformation that would make her life a living testimony to His kingdom.

When Mary was sitting by Him listening, Jesus said of her, "Mary has chosen the better part" (Luke 10:42, NRSVCE), as her sister Martha pressed for help with household needs. What He was sharing with Mary, and she was receiving, was worth everything in the world— yet nothing on earth could buy it. It may be that Jesus was not simply referring to a way of life that was better but also to a disposition of the heart. At the root of Mary's transformative action was her *being* with Him. Hearing His words, both gentle and challenging, and sitting in the silence with Him were filling the emptiness of what He had expelled from her.

INVITATION

- Transformation in Christ requires courage, allowing the Lord access to strip away what is false. Silent prayer is imperative for lasting freedom. In Eucharistic adoration we know that "before his gaze all falsehood melts away. This encounter with him, as it burns us, transforms and frees us, allowing us to become truly ourselves."[2] Are there struggles that I am attached to? Do I really desire transformation? Do I trust that in letting the inauthentic part of me die, the Lord will fill my truest self so that all may know "I have seen the Lord"?

- There are no sins beyond God's mercy. Do I go to the Sacrament of Confession *with trust* that Jesus can break bondage and heal? Jesus said to St. Faustina, specifically of Confession, "There the greatest miracles take place, are incessantly repeated,"[3] and, "Tell souls that from this fount of mercy souls draw graces solely with the vessel of trust. If their trust is great, there is no limit to My generosity."[4] Am I aiming only to be free of sin, or am I asking Lord for the virtues that oppose my struggles?

- Is there a saint who had similar struggles as me? Can I look to their example and call on their

2 Benedict XVI, Encyclical Letter on Christian Hope *Spe Salvi* (November 30, 2007), §47 (hereafter cited in text as SS).

3 Kowalska, *Diary of St. Faustina*, para. 1448.

4 Kowalska, *Diary of St. Faustina*, para. 1602.

intercession to help me trust the power of God's transforming love?

DAY 18

That not knowing what tomorrow brings is an invitation to lean on You, Jesus, I trust in You.

We all know what we want for tomorrow—we want *more*. More of whatever goodness we had today, plus . . . *more*. What is that "more," specifically?

Steve worked many years in a job he was not passionate about, only to switch to another job that seemed to be going nowhere. Married with five children, he took a leap of faith to move to an area close to family, with many connections to promising job opportunities. It was a great location, but the stress increased as each potential job surprisingly fell through. Weeks turned into months, and Steve would lie awake at night holding his crucifix and begging the Lord for help. He felt he had no other place to lean. He had applied to a wide variety of jobs but still nothing materialized.

One day he spoke to his parish priest, who suggested that every morning as soon as he woke up, he should thank God for the amazing job He was going to provide for him and his family. His daily prayers were now imbued with a trusting gratitude for a God who loved him and knew what he needed. Finally, a friend reached out to him, securing an interview for him for a job that far exceeded his requests. Hired on the spot, Steve realized God had had this in mind all along. And an entire year of anguish had won a trust in his heart that would never leave him. The trial had turned into a gift.

The Blessed Virgin Mary, when a mere teenager, heard the angel Gabriel announcing that she would be the mother of God. Every "tomorrow" would be dramatically different. Mary recognized the grandeur and mystery of Christ's life growing within her and met it with a deep reverence. She must have marveled in awe while also feeling at a loss for how she would live this call day to day. Though she did not know the future, she was able to rest knowing Jesus was in it.

We can learn from Mary to likewise be reverent toward the mystery of Christ's presence in our life. *Christ*—present in *my* life. His life is growing within me. How am I going to live henceforth? Am I going to seek what He desires and allow Him to lead the way? Like the Blessed Virgin Mary, we cannot see the future, but we can trust that Jesus is in it.

As Steve was confident that God had provided this job for him, a new invitation to renew that trust was given as difficulties arose in the job. Knowing he could have gotten plenty of other jobs, it was clear this too was a part of God asking him to draw close, yet again. To live in trust is to move toward God when we don't know which way to go. And, in faith, to allow the goodness of God to bring us to gratitude even before God reveals His plan. Trust rests knowing that God is leading.

JESUS, I TRUST IN YOU

The night before His Passion, when the air was thick with anticipation for the morrow, there was one who followed the inspiration of the Holy Spirit boldly and leaned on the side of Christ (John 13:23). This disciple, John, did not know how things would transpire in the upcoming days and felt their magnitude as tensions were rising against Jesus.

Being in Jesus' presence, John must have experienced an overwhelming admiration for Him. The way Jesus spoke, looked into his eyes, the way He lived so freely . . . He exceeded John's understanding. In his love for Jesus, John stopped trying to grasp everything about Jesus and the prophecies of His upcoming death, and simply decided to be devoted to Him. Instead of being caught up in fears of what the trials ahead may be, John saw that this night held something sacred to Jesus, and he did not want to miss it.

Jesus was consoled by John's attentive trust. There, Jesus stood on the brink of the most intense day of His thirty-three years on earth. Gathered with those He called to be with Him, He must have noticed that many were distracted by their anxiety, because we hear Jesus say, "Peace I leave with you; my peace I give to you; not as the world gives do I give to you. Let not your hearts be troubled, neither let them be afraid" (John 14:27).

Yet John's availability in his openness of heart, despite all the pressing concerns, was a place of rest for Jesus. In John, Jesus knew He was seen. Even the dramatic troubles of the following day would not deter John from his decision to stay near Jesus. John would follow Jesus to the high priest's house and Pilate's courtyard, on the road to Calvary, and beneath the Cross. John was learning the truth that uncertainties would come and go, as well as the challenges they would entail, but the Lord is unchanging. And through it all, Jesus was impressing on John a trust that with Him all would be well.

INVITATION

• Like John, when we are fearful of the unknown road ahead, may we never lose sight of what Jesus is offering us: a place close to His heart. It is far better for us to live in the vulnerability of letting go of our timeline, to receive Him meeting us in time. When we feel impatient or start micromanaging our lives, can we ask for reverence, which allows whatever is before me to unfold, rather than grasping to control it? How is Jesus asking me to lean on Him?

• Our prayer and attitude toward God can begin to get scrappy when we have lost a sense of gratitude for who He is. He wants to provide, especially in times when we are bogged down by uncertainty. When worries mount, can we pause to thank God in advance for what He will bring forth?

• The peace Jesus offers is not a peace that the world offers, which seems contingent on our plans falling into place. The peace He gives is sturdier, coming from the confidence that the unchanging God is with us. If I lose my peace every time I watch the news or read the paper, can I limit myself to that which is truly necessary, rather than being caught up in the frenzy? Turn what you hear into an opportunity for intercessory prayer.

DAY 19

That You are with me in my suffering, Jesus, I trust in You.

In the midst of life's sufferings, it is the great tactic of the evil one to persuade us that we are alone. Possibly forgotten. This deception of isolation only adds a deeper layer to our pain. Many think that Jesus only suffers with the saints and not with those of us who are struggling along the way. This is not true. Jesus meets us personally in our sufferings, with the reverence of a privileged friend on sacred ground. And He comes with the invitation to make our suffering illuminated with love, ultimately transforming suffering in this life to the invaluable: union with God. As we grow in our relationship with Christ, that intimacy with Him in our suffering likewise grows. He is with us all the while.

When I suffer the pain of physical ailments, the false accusations of others, or any number of difficulties, He is with me. Not staring blankly at me, but embracing me. Jesus does not belittle my pain or get fatigued by it. As Savior, Jesus is drawn to me in my suffering. Even when my suffering is a direct effect of deliberately going against His commandments—such as losing my job because I was dishonest—Jesus knows the deeper pain of my heart that prompted my choice and continues to make Himself available. It is in the midst of suffering that many people meet Christ for the first time, whether or not they've been going to church for years.

By earning a doctorate in philosophy in 1916, Edith Stein was, as a woman, far ahead of her time. What fueled her passion was a quest for truth. Her greatest lessons, however, would be outside the classroom on her journey from Judaism and atheism to Catholicism, from living for herself to dying for her people. One of these experiences came through visiting a Christian friend, Anna Reinach, after Anna's husband, a beloved teacher of Edith's, had passed away. Edith was awed by Anna's undeniable peace in the midst of her grief. "It was my first encounter with the cross and the divine power that it bestows on those who carry it. For the first time I was seeing with my very eyes the church, born from its Redeemer's sufferings, triumphant over the sting of death.... That was the moment my unbelief collapsed."[1] She had encountered Christ, so present in the sufferings of her friend.

The Cross of Christ was the point of departure for her Jewish brethren but a new place of blessing for Edith. Christ's Passion led her not only to become a Carmelite sister but to see His sacrifice as the decisive moment of history, pervading every moment of life. Without Christ's triumph over suffering and death on the Cross, we would have been left hopelessly alone to suffer the devastating effects of sin. But with it, He now stands in the midst of every sorrow, offering the strength He won on the Cross to transform it to a place of eternal love.

So when Edith Stein, who later became Sr. Teresa

---

[1] Waltraud Herbstrith, *Edith Stein: A Biography* (San Francisco: Ignatius Press, 1985), 56.

Benedicta of the Cross, was arrested by the Nazis because of her Jewish heritage, she accepted it. Because of Christ's victory on the Cross, she could now see this suffering as it was—an opportunity to join Christ, communicating His love to the world in the fullest way. As they arrived at the concentration camp, eyewitnesses share that as she stepped off the train, she was seen holding the hands of children whose parents were either not present or paralyzed by fear. She was combing their hair and caring for them, calmly leading them in prayer. Although she could not take away their suffering, she was able to be with them in it.

Wherever we find ourselves, whether we are coping with someone we love being in the throes of an addiction, or dreading another day of negativity at work, or strapped in a financial crisis, we have access to another whose love redefines our messy world. The heart of one who trusts the presence of Jesus in suffering engages the power of His Cross, which frees us from burdens that we were never intended to carry and strengthens us to carry those that remain, with love and even joy.

Edith could see this in her own life. The death of her father when she was young, the frustrations of not being able to get a position as a female professor even though she was qualified, the painful reaction of her mother when she became Catholic, and most especially her last trial of being innocently put to death had all been places God had been powerfully present. Initially she only saw the pain in suffering, but when she encountered a God who Himself suffered, she was drawn out of her isolated independence, seeing everything past, present, and future as her being conformed to Christ through His

Cross. Trusting His love freed her to live her deepest desire: giving her life as Jesus did. Trust receives suffering as Jesus' longing to be with me.

JESUS, I TRUST IN YOU

Walking together on that first Easter Sunday, two disciples left Jerusalem for the town of Emmaus. Their hearts were heavy and confused as they tried to make sense of what had happened. Jesus, whom they had hoped would be the king of Israel, was put to death. And that day they had heard reports that He was seen, risen from the dead. As they discussed this, "Jesus himself drew near and went with them" (Luke 24:15), although they did not know who He was. Listening to them, He brought light to the anguish of their hearts. "Did not our hearts burn within us while he talked to us on the road" (Luke 24:32)? When they reached Emmaus, the destination of the two disciples, Jesus made it seem like He was continuing on His journey. It was as though He, who purposefully had accompanied them all the while, longed to see if they likewise desired His company. After they urged Jesus to stay with them, He accepted. And then, in the breaking of the bread, they recognized Him.

Jesus is on the road with us, even if we are walking away from Jerusalem, as these disciples were. He wants to hear from our lips the reasons we too may doubt God when suffering hits. Grappling with their disappointment, these followers of Jesus shared that their image of a messiah was not one that suffered and died. We wonder what the full content was that Jesus spoke to light their hearts on fire in response to their bewilderment.

However, we do hear that Jesus mentioned it was "necessary that the Christ should suffer these things and enter into his glory" (Luke 24:26). It is striking that He used the word "necessary." This suffering, which so baffled them, was the actual hinge of Jesus' triumph. It was *the* means through which Jesus would choose to be united to us forever, if we accepted. The true Messiah was with His people and for His people, necessarily in the place of suffering, to free them from the inside out. In bearing our infirmities, as the suffering-servant prophecy in Isaiah foretells, He is with us and victorious (Isa 53:4–5, 10–12).

INVITATION

- When suffering hits, we might wonder if we deserve it, and God is somehow punishing us. Or if others in our life have walked away in times of our suffering, it can be hard to believe that Almighty God would desire to be with us in our deepest burdens. What is my image of a messiah, a savior, . . . God? Am I opening my heart to Christ in the big and the small crosses I carry? Or am I closing my heart in distrust by avoiding Jesus?

- In my suffering can I, like the disciples, beg Jesus to stay with me—even before I recognize His presence with me? Had the disciples not invited Jesus to stay with them, they would have never realized who was with them. Bring your suffering to the Mass and spiritually place it on the altar so that it may be offered in union with Jesus' sacrifice on the Cross. This will fill it with the victory He won for us and open our hearts in faith to recognize Him with us.

- Do I have a blessed crucifix in my room or in a prominent place in my house? The purpose of a crucifix is not to deny the Resurrection of Jesus but to proclaim the love that is freely offered to us in every moment, which nothing can destroy. Turning to the crucifix, ask for a greater openness to the love He is pouring out for you in your suffering.

That my suffering, united to Your own, will bear fruit in this life and the next, Jesus, I trust in You.

By choosing to suffer, Jesus has given suffering an inestimable value. Even the smallest pain united to His suffering will be a jewel for all eternity. The discomfort passes, but the love that we pour out through it endures forever.

Do I want my life to be fruitful, to go beyond myself and inspire a lasting good in other lives? To help others live forever with God? What could be of greater consequence? This is God's plan. But the love that precedes the fruitfulness is what God so desires and (like all loves) must come first. In this broken world we can be scared to trust that love, so we more easily settle for what does not endure. Instead of refusing a job that compromises the living of my faith, I accept it, thinking about the extra income I can do good with; meanwhile, the source of fruitfulness, intimacy with God, is conceded.

What often holds us back from this intimacy with Christ is that we fear suffering, especially when it seems meaningless. We avoid traffic at all costs, take medicine at the first tinge of pain, or cross to the opposite side of the street when we see a homeless person. While it is not sinful to lessen pain and it is part of charity to lessen suffering for others, suffering is inevitable. In fact, we often choose to suffer for things we deem worthy. Wearing top-of-the-line shoes that are wildly uncomfortable is worthwhile for one who is hungry to be noticed. Sacrificing amusements to spend more time studying is desirable to those who want to excel. Much of the suffering that is *willingly* endured in our culture is spent on loving ourselves. Something of suffering's immense value is lost in this, however. When love is turned outward to serve the true good of another, and most powerfully when we live that courageous love for God, a tremendous fruitfulness emerges.

In the 1980s, tensions were mounting in Poland as the Soviet party was repressing the solidarity movement and as martial law was declared. The young Fr. Jerzy Popiełuszko was assigned to say Mass for the solidarity movement workers in Warsaw. He was chosen well, for he was no stranger to standing up for what he loved. Prior to his ordination, he was drafted for a two-year military service. There, he was ridiculed and so badly beaten for praying the rosary that he had to have surgery to repair the damage done to his heart and kidneys. And now, in Warsaw as a spiritual father in the midst of injustice, he did not back down, knowing what it might cost him. He had a love worth fighting for and would do so without using physical force or violence. Instead he intensified his prayer life and celebrated monthly "Masses for the Homeland," where hundreds of thousands would gather to receive spiritual strength, to keep their hearts and hope alive. In Fr. Popiełuszko's words,

We fear suffering; we fear the loss of some goods, the loss of freedom, health or job. This fear makes us act against our conscience and it is by means of conscience that we measure Truth. We overcome fear the moment we agree to lose something for the sake of higher values. If Truth becomes a value worth suffering for, worth taking a risk, then we will overcome fear that keeps us in slavery. On many occasions Christ said to His apostles: "Do not fear. Do not fear those who kill the body and after that have no more that they can do" (Lk 12:4).[1]

When Fr. Jerzy was ambushed and killed for what he proclaimed, the country mourned, but no one took up arms. They had truly come to know, through him, the unstoppable quality of love that suffers for the truth. His life was evidence that "the capacity to accept suffering for the sake of goodness, truth, and justice is an essential criterion of humanity, because if my own well-being and safety are ultimately more important than truth and justice, then the power of the stronger prevails, then violence and untruth reign supreme" (SS 38).

Don't avoid suffering, but avoid suffering *uselessly*. Especially in situations where we are asked to suffer for the sake of truth, much can be gained. Jesus shows us that suffering united to Him is the path to life, for ourselves and countless others. Jesus' suffering saved the world, as through it He offered Himself to the Father for our sake. Now, Jesus asks us to trust in the priceless

[1] Fr. Jerzy Popiełuszko, Homily from "Mass for the Homeland" (October 1982), https://catholic-link.org/jerzy-popieluszko.

quality of allowing His loving gift to the Father to be lived in me and overflow to others. Trust sees, through the wounds of Christ, the abundance of life offered to me and others in my sufferings.

JESUS, I TRUST IN YOU

Jesus suffered for what He loved. You. And me. Love impelled Him to bring us back into relationship with Him, to restore us to our heavenly heritage. The Sunday before He died, many were gathered for a feast in Jerusalem. As Jesus arrived, many of the Jews hailed Him as King because they had just witnessed Him raising Lazarus from the dead.

But mixed in the crowd were also some Greeks, who said to the apostle Philip, "Sir, we wish to see Jesus" (John 12:21). It was known that Jews seek signs and Greeks seek wisdom (1 Cor 1:22), so when the apostles shared this request with Jesus, He responded, "[U]nless a grain of wheat falls into the earth and dies, it remains alone; but if it dies, it bears much fruit" (John 12:24). This was the wisdom Jesus wanted to convey: to see Him one must have the eyes to see what the world gazes right past—the hidden truth of all true life. The seed of self-sacrifice given for love of others allows new life to mysteriously emerge.

On the Cross, where Jesus wanted to be seen, He cried out, "My God, my God, why have you forsaken me?" (Matt 27:46). With these jarring words, was not Jesus communicating being plunged into the depths of the sorrow of our sin and our forsakenness, like the seed in the darkness of earth? Yet in this experience of extreme anguish, He still trusted the Father, infusing into the farthest reaches of human isolation His very own life-giving intimacy with the Father. For Psalm 22 (which Jesus was quoting on the Cross) continues, "In you our fathers trusted; they trusted, and you delivered them" (v. 4). The psalm ends victorious: "May your hearts live for ever! . . . men shall tell of the Lord to the coming generation, and proclaim his deliverance to a people yet unborn, that he has wrought it" (vv. 26, 30–31). His trusting love was already claiming the generations of people who would receive the new life brought in this suffering.

The most healing thing Jesus did for us was die on the Cross. And He invites us to receive healing through the carrying of our cross, in union with Him. For it is in this that we most powerfully know the truth of His wisdom: "He who abides in me, and I in him, he it is that bears much fruit, for apart from me you can do nothing" (John 15:5).

INVITATION

- We each have a decision to make in our suffering: to live it for love of another or not. Do I know what I am willing to suffer for? Take some time to put before the Lord the suffering of your life and ask if you have taken it upon yourself, or if He is inviting you to a deeper love through it. We can put an intention on our suffering, interceding for others and those we love. "Offer it up" is a phrase commonly used to encourage someone to give their suffering worth. A short way to do this is by praying throughout my day, "Jesus, I unite myself to You. And I offer up my sufferings for _____."

• God intends to bless the suffering He allows with specific fruit—it has a positive effect on my life and others, even though we often don't see the fruit of our suffering. Although it is like a seed hidden in the earth, we can trust the Lord to make it "spring up." Every morning, start the day with a prayer that unites your day with Jesus'. Then, nothing will be wasted, but it will be joined with His love and multiplied. The Morning Offering prayer is a simple way to do this and can be placed at your bedside. "O Jesus, through the Immaculate Heart of Mary, I offer You my prayers, works, joys, and sufferings of this day for all the intentions of Your Sacred Heart, in union with the Holy Sacrifice of the Mass throughout the world, for the salvation of souls, the reparation of sins, the reunion of all Christians, and in particular for the intentions of the Holy Father this month. Amen."

• Fear holds us back from accepting the crosses in life that He allows, which are meant to not only bear fruit for all eternity but to prepare us to see Him in heaven. Our sufferings in this life are allowed as a type of mercy, to heal us by removing all that is not of God in our hearts. Purgatory, where one goes after death if it is still necessary to be purified for heaven, is a continuation of this mercy of

God. However, we are all in need of purification at some point; let's do it now, when others can be brought to love through our sufferings, rather than after death, when our purification only benefits us. Where is fear holding me back from receiving the graces hidden in suffering?

DAY 21

That You will not leave me orphan, that You are present in Your Church, Jesus, I trust in You.

Jesus did not want to leave us orphans (John 14:18) but assured us that we would always have a home to turn to, no matter what conditions we found ourselves in. Derived from the Greek *Kyriake*, the word "church" means "what belongs to the Lord" (CCC 751).

Jesus established the Church to continue to preach and uphold this good news He proclaimed and to make Himself present for generations to come, that all who believe would find salvation through union with Him. The Church bespeaks the desire of God, that we begin to live more fully His divine life. We are meant to rest in our belonging to Him, in and through the Church.

But we can struggle to trust this promise of the Lord, when the broken and sinful realities so visible in the Church leave us wondering if God is present. Have we been left on our own? How can a wounded Church be a *source* of grace and divine life? Trust has been abused by many of those who promise to uphold it. And so there arises, in justice, an outcry of scandal, as countless hearts have been shattered by those in the Church who lived contrary to the teachings of Christ.

This is the mystery of the Cross. The Church is, in a real and mystical way, the Body of Christ—the very body of Christ that hung upon the Cross, rose from the dead, and reigns now in heaven. By becoming members of the Church, we receive Christ's identity as our own, and are incorporated into His saving death and Resurrection, to live with Him forever. His life becomes ours. The Church "gathers together to form the People of God, and who themselves, nourished with the Body of Christ, become the Body of Christ" (CCC 777). Our wounds are His. He Himself is wounded by the sins of the Church.

Mary's perspective can help us see Christ's presence in a human Church. She never doubted Jesus' presence, as true God and true man, as He hung battered and reviled on the Cross. His body bore the scourges, yet nothing could eclipse the heavenly reality of His undying love. Mary saw the divine in a messy place, and she was able to enter into it. Here, at the foot of the Cross, it pierced every part of her to know that He was completely innocent yet suffered the rejection of a dangerous criminal. Instead of being bitter against the very people who were perpetrating this evil against her son, she knew it was for love of them that her son was giving His life. Thus, as both mother to her son *and* to those who put Him to death—for Jesus gives Mary as mother to all people—she suffers with Christ to intercede that all may know the love that is offered to them. Suffering with Christ, she has become one with her son, and likewise shares His mission of laboring to love the very ones who pierce His and her hearts. She sees not just a wounded presence but an eternal presence.

Jesus Christ and the Church are one. Choosing to

establish the Church is how Jesus chose to communicate Himself. That is why, even with the extensive brokenness of its members, the Church still remains irreplaceable. We need the Church precisely *because* of our human frailty. We all need the mercy of God, that unconditional love from Jesus' death given so explicitly in and through the sacraments of the Church. Where else can one go when looking for forgiveness and sturdy hope? Our God is big enough to make a lot of wrongs right—not in justifying evil but in bringing a love that is greater than evil. No one is an outcast in God's eyes.

Bartolo Longo was born into an Italian Catholic family, but by the time he was in law school, he had completely abandoned the faith of his childhood. The death of his mother at an early age, then some years later his father, left him drifting into the world of spiritualism. Along with many of his classmates, he began attending seances and orgies, as well as publicly mocking the Catholic Church. He convinced many Catholics to leave the Church, he himself becoming a satanic priest. He hated the pope, the saints, and all that the Church stood for. During all of this, he battled intense bouts of confusion and sadness.

One day he heard the voice of his deceased father call out to him, "Return to God!" Although not easily disturbed, Bartolo was shaken up. He went to a priest, who took Bartolo under his wing. The priest showed him that it was only because the Catholic Church is so unified with Christ that Satan directly mimicked and attacked it. The following weeks set him on a radical new trajectory as he returned to the sacraments of the Church.

Moved by the conditions of the physically and spiritually poor in Pompeii, Bartolo wanted to help create what he had so keenly found in the Church: a *home*. Knowing the pain of losing both parents, he started to care for orphaned children and children of prisoners, and also committed to building a large Catholic church in the neighborhood, so all people could encounter the Father who lived among them. Bartolo placed all his work under the patronage of the Blessed Mother, praying the rosary in thanksgiving for her intercession in reviving his soul. Feeling so disconnected all those years of his youth, Bartolo now knew that he had, in fact, never been left alone.[1]

While it may happen that we struggle to trust in Christ's presence in the Church, because of the sins or weaknesses of its members, walking away from the Church is ultimately about not trusting God's mercy. If I dismiss the Church because of its brokenness, I may also be dismissing the real call in my life toward wholeness—which necessitates receiving His mercy when I do not feel worthy of it. God is continually faithful to us in making Himself vulnerable in the sacraments, even while Himself suffering abuse, as Bartolo's former life of sacrilege attests. If we fail to recognize this, we risk never knowing the true home of His mercy.

JESUS, I TRUST IN YOU

The Church was God's idea. Jesus is the one who speaks of it and founds it on Peter's confession of faith. For as

---

[1] Ann Ball, "Blessed Bartolo Longo (1841–1926)," chap. 36 in *Modern Saints*, bk. 2.

Peter professes that Jesus is the Christ, the Son of the Living God, Jesus makes His declaration, "And I tell you, you are Peter, and on this rock I will build my church, and the gates of hell shall not prevail against it" (Matt 16:18, ESV).

And hell has tried. Satan did not wait even a minute, as the following verses tell of Peter pulling Jesus aside to scold Him, saying that He will *not* suffer and die. Jesus calls him out, saying, "Get behind me, Satan!" (Matt 16:23). Peter was not thinking as God does but as man does, lacking the supernatural vision of faith. Jesus does not retract His earlier proclamation to Peter but affirms it. Since Peter is now a member of the Church, which is Christ's Mystical Body, Peter is being called to love both Him *and* those for whom Jesus will give the gift of His life.

When Jesus is asked by Jews for a sign that they might believe in Him, mentioning that the Israelites received manna from heaven to sustain them on their journey to the promised land, Jesus gives them an unexpected response. He says, "I am the living bread which came down from heaven; if any one eats of this bread, he will live forever; and the bread which I shall give for the life of the world is my flesh" (John 6:51). In disbelief, they question what Jesus says, only to hear Him say more clearly, "He who eats my flesh and drinks my blood abides in me, and I in him" (v. 56). Jesus chose to nourish us with His Body and Blood—not only so that we can reach the promised land of heaven, but so that we can abide in Him and He in us.

The Church, as His Body, is the place where the sharing of His divine life is ensured through the sacraments, the continual giving and reception of His flesh for the life of the world. He wants to personally come to every land and nation, in every time and place, particularly in the Eucharist.

In His love for all, Jesus does not excuse those who veer off the path, or pretend scandal does not seriously hurt us and others (Luke 17:1–2). He corrects in order to heal. He alone can make new what is shattered (Rev 21:5), inviting each to a life-giving repentance through the authority of the Church, which brings us back onto the path.

INVITATION

• Jesus invites us to love as members of His Body. Like the Blessed Mother at the foot of the Cross, we are called to love both Jesus *and* those He gave His life for (including myself). By loving the members of His Body, I am loving Jesus. Am I even aware that Jesus is in His members? When faced with annoyance, hypocrisy, or scandal, do I trust that Jesus can give me the grace to love the members of the Body? The only way it is possible is through Jesus' very own love, given to us in the Eucharist.

• Do I pray for the Church? Do I pray for the Holy Father, cardinals, bishops, priests, and religious? My own parish? It can be as simple as saying an Our Father every time we pass a church or hear the steeple bells toll, or at a specified time every day.

We can also ask for a greater love for the Church, and for the graces we've received in Baptism and other sacraments to be stirred up.

• The gift of a well-catechized mind can be helpful for recognizing sound teaching and integrating it into your life. However, when you find yourself confused and tempted to become your own authority, deciding what you think is best, you are treading on thin ice, sliding away from Christ. Am I taking on the burden of authority actually entrusted to Peter, or am I receiving the teachings of the Church in good faith?

Day 22

That Your plan is better than anything else, Jesus, I trust in You.

I grew up in a home where my parents knew that only God could have brought them together. Every day we said three Hail Marys for divine providence, asking God to continue to provide for our family. Through my parents' witness, I have come to see that God's plan is far more personal than I would have expected.

My father grew up in New York City, the son of Italian immigrants. His father worked hard and unfortunately spent little time with the family. The oldest child, Daniel, had a psychotic break in his teens and was diagnosed with schizophrenia when my dad was only in middle school. Tension and sadness filled the home as they struggled to find solutions. The years ahead were spent adjusting to their radically different family life and clinging to faith despite the unanswered questions and pain. This new direction impelled my father to study medicine in Italy and provided the opportunity in 1966 to visit Padre Pio, a Franciscan priest who had many mystical gifts.

At the friary church, he met my mother, who was from Germany and was also on pilgrimage to see Padre

Pio. Suffering had likewise chiseled her path to this point. Seeking to spend more time with the Lord, whose love was filling her heart, my mother was drawn to pray at the Capuchin church of Padre Pio. Upon meeting one another, my father sensed this was the woman he was going to marry. It would later be confirmed when he asked Padre Pio's advice in Confession, and he said "Marry her!"

I often think about what would have happened if my dad had stopped praying during his youth and pushed God aside instead of seeking His will. Or if my mom had been resistant to the healing graces of His love, so needed after the devastating betrayals in her family. Or what if Padre Pio had not said as generous of a "yes" to God's call to holiness and simply been a mediocre priest? It was only his profound holiness that could radiate his fatherhood so widely, especially to those in need of a spiritual father.

God had arranged everything. And continues to. When we are overwhelmed by the details of our lives and can think of a thousand other creative ways things could work out differently, it is hard to believe God is actually devising the optimal plan for us. But trust enables us to be confident that God is always at work to give us the best plan for our wholeness and holiness.

While my parents did not know how the messy start to their young lives could be made good, they knew only God could accomplish it. And they never regretted trusting Him.

God's plan for each of us is to be drawn up into His love and to witness His love to the world. Thus it will always be better than what we can devise or create.

When we are tempted to think, "God forgot about me," or, "I missed my chance to live His plan," we can remember that His love is always accessible and His plan starts from right where we are.

JESUS, I TRUST IN YOU

Jesus spent His earthly life following the plan of the Father. While He was attending a wedding feast in Cana with His mother and disciples, Mary approached Jesus to tell Him that the wedding couple had run out of wine for their guests. Since Jesus had performed no miracles openly before, doing a miracle here would mark a definitive beginning to His public mission that would culminate on the Cross. Knowing this, Jesus responds to her plea by saying, "O woman, what have you to do with me? My hour has not yet come" (John 2:4).

The conversation seems to continue more in looks and an interior knowledge of the heart than in words. Mary, in hearing Jesus' response, must have received it with a validating confidence, knowing what He meant by calling her "woman."

Use of the word "woman" harkens back to Genesis, where in God's perfect plan, He created Adam and Eve to share in His love. God commanded them, made in His image, to be "fruitful and multiply," thus sharing in the creativity of His love (Gen 1:28). This plan for Adam and Eve necessitated one another. Individually and united, each was integral to revealing God's love in the world. Adam, initially alone, could not live this mission of revealing God's love to the world. God chose that in woman's very person, she would usher into creation a love that breaks open the mystery of heaven. For only in light of one another do man and woman come to a true sense of identity, as an extension of God's very love.

Hence, by being called "woman," Mary becomes the New Eve. So Mary, with full trust in Jesus' love for her and in her critical role in His mission—different yet complementary—turns to the waiters and says, "Do whatever he tells you" (John 2:5). She breaks open this heavenly mission of love in Jesus for all to see, knowing that there would be rich and abundant wine, an expression of the call "to be fruitful and multiply." Jesus, as the New Adam, sees that He is not alone in accomplishing His mission. The love between them overflows as the waiters likewise trust Jesus and fill six jugs with water at His request. He, who has been drawn out by this woman to manifest the love of God, instructs the waiters regarding the water that is now wine: they are to "draw some out" to bring to the steward of the celebration (v. 8). Jesus wants it to be savored, shared, and pronounced as good (v. 10). Here, a wine is tasted that is far better than what the wedding couple could have procured.

Our God, who is Triune, has a plan for each of us to manifest His love to the world. Since God has chosen to reveal His love through masculinity and femininity, it is essential that we trust who He has created us to be, as man or woman, in order to truly abide in His life. And the magnificence of masculinity and femininity is that they are ordered toward being drawn out of ourselves in love. Even broader than a sexual love, man and woman uniquely show forth traits of God's very own heart.

Both Jesus and Mary chose to live fully their God-given identities. Because of that, from the deficit of wine at Cana emerged a fruitful love, surpassing the best of human provisions. In the lack we may experience from our own parents' failings or weaknesses—despite their best intentions—the love between Jesus and Mary provides exceedingly. For we are that water-made-wine, the fruit of the love between the New Adam and New Eve that affirms that God's plan is perfect for us, from our creation to our new creation in His grace.

INVITATION

- Those three Hail Marys for divine providence went a long way for my family: God provided physically and spiritually, from college education to the graces of faith in each of us. He wants to provide for us better than our human efforts alone can afford. As I pray for His plan to be lived in me, am I willing to "do whatever He tells me," beginning with being faithful in small matters?

- God desires us to witness His love to the world. Looking to Jesus and Mary, we can ask them to draw out the true gift of ourselves in love, so that all may be abundantly blessed through it. Am I witnessing God's love to the world?

- It can be attractive to walk away from what is difficult in life and "start over" on our own. Instead of quitting something, God may desire to provide new wine right there. This is especially true when a definitive commitment has been made. Do I trust that God's plan is truly the best and can be accessed right where I'm at? Ask for the grace of the waiters at the wedding feast of Cana, to not only fill the jugs at His word, but to fill them "up to the brim" (John 2:7).

That You always hear me and in Your goodness always respond to me, Jesus, I trust in You.

One afternoon, several of my Sisters and I had the chance to go to a large museum in New York City. We wound up at a space exhibit, where an older gentleman walked up to us with a large pin on his blazer that read "Volunteer Explainer." He asked us if we had any questions about the galaxies or what they held. It was an opportunity we couldn't pass up and we began inquiring about black holes. He seemed to have his data down but alluded to the fact that there was still so much to be known. Noticing how his eyes brimmed with curiosity seeing religious Sisters in front of him, one of the Sisters took the conversation deeper and said, "What happens when the data can't explain something? Who do *you* ask to get answers?" And refusing to reply, he shook his head and walked away.

Even though we were no longer in it, I do hope that conversation continued. Whether we realize it or not, there is someone who hears and responds—the one who holds all creation in His hands.

Just like the vast galaxies, there is so much we don't see and don't know about ourselves and about God. And one of the things we can wonder is if my prayers are being received or if they are getting lost in the black holes of space. Sometimes we mention something to God, and soon after it is answered in the way we asked; and then other times, it seems like there is no response at all. It can make us question if our previous experiences were just coincidences or simply figments of our imagination.

God is always answering *us*. As we raise a petition to Him, He not only hears the words but also receives us and wants us to know through His response that He is giving us what is best for our eternal life. He responds to us *as a person*, not to mere words, as if he were a volunteer explainer.

Some people always answer their phone when we call. They are available and reliable, and we love it. We can easily stop sharing things that really matter with a person who does not seem available or dependable to us, those who say one thing and act in another way. If this is how we see God, we no longer pray to God, thinking He is not worthy of our trust. Undeterred, God's light is always on, laboring to meet our every need. Trust knows that God hears every movement of my heart and is waiting to meet me there.

What, then, is God's seeming silence? First, we must ask ourselves if we are truly open to listening. If we are strongly attached to our plans or struggling with serious sin, our hearing can be blocked. Even so, an honest desire to authentically hear His word can illuminate the next step on the path.

Secondly, silence can be an invitation of God drawing someone deeper. He is present in the longing we experience in silence. Words, and even felt experience, are a limited expression of God, who is far bigger than these things. He wants you to get to know Him, in and through silence. It is a kind of hiddenness that is necessary for intimacy to grow; a hiddenness because there is something good and He wants you to come closer to Him as He reveals it. He asks us to listen in a new way, trusting that letting go of our own concepts of His voice and attentiveness will allow things to unfold in His hands. We can pray, pray, pray for healing, and then when it doesn't come, we think God is not listening. But then one day we are struck at our progress and realize He's been at it all along. The very holding of our hearts is His continual response.

JESUS, I TRUST IN YOU

Jesus wants us to tell Him what is on our hearts and He does not tire of reminding us. "Ask, and it will be given you; seek, and you will find; knock, and it will be opened to you" (Matt 7:7); and "pray to your Father who is in secret; and your Father who sees in secret will reward you" (Matt 6:6). Jesus Himself made efforts to step away from the disciples in order to have time alone to pray to His heavenly Father (Matt 14:13; Luke 6:12).

An occasion that may make us wonder about how Jesus responds to the petitions of our hearts is that of Lazarus' sickness. The Gospels do not tell us much more about Lazarus than that Jesus loved him and his sisters: Martha and, some scholars believe, Mary Magdalene (John 11:5). The sisters had sent word to Jesus, asking

Him to heal their brother, Lazarus, since they knew
Jesus had done this for many others. However, there
was no answer until four days after Lazarus died. Upon
Jesus' arrival, He weeps for his friend. He feels the ter-
rible emptiness of earth without him. Aware that those
present doubted His goodness to them, He approaches
Lazarus' tomb, praying aloud, "Father, I thank you that
you have heard me. I [know] that you always hear me"
(John 11:41–42). Beckoning Lazarus to come out, the
dead man arises, causing the hearts of many to believe in
Him.

This family that Jesus loved was learning that Jesus
was not like anyone else they knew. They could not
compare Him to others. What Jesus decided to do and
say was worthy of respect, simply because He was the
Son of the Living God. As such, He was teaching them
to trust His intentions. Why He did not come and cure
Lazarus right away seemed bizarre and hard to understand, but as they would see, Jesus allowed the Father to
lead Him to a greater design.

It would only be a week later that Mary would find
herself at another tomb (John 20:1), this time clinging in faith to the promise her heart must have made
the day of Lazarus' return: that she would never doubt
Jesus again. Although things could not have looked
darker than Jesus' cruel death, she would not let go of
His promise of resurrection, even though it would defy
natural explanations—He must be up to something.
And coming to her that Easter morning, Jesus sought
to reward that trust of her heart, which in her eyes felt
fragile, but in His eyes was fierce. Mary Magdalene had
unshakeable trust in Jesus' love for her, knowing that

He would hear her and respond to her. And calling her name—"Mary"—Jesus did.

INVITATION

- Silence in our relationship with God enables a purity of simply *being* with Him. Without words or specific thoughts, He is able to communicate with us. Am I willing to give Him the benefit of the doubt when His response seems lacking to me? Do I believe that God's intentions are good? Or, perhaps, am I praying for things that God may not want for me?

- Jesus asks us to pray in His name. In this He shares with us the privileged place of intercession that He has with the Father (John 14:13), as He prays "in our place and on our behalf" (CCC 2741). And praying with this confidence opens our hearts to more readily receive what He wants to give us. How do I share my needs and desires with God?

- We hear that "tax collectors and sinners were all drawing near to hear him" (Luke 15:1). All of us are capable of hearing Jesus and receiving His guidance. The following is a quote that can encourage us on the right path:

  > Search, scour, dig, beg God to make you more conscious not only of his presence, but . . . of being more sure I am not only

talking to God but He's talking to me. The last thing we should do is to distrust the insights, the ideas, the impulses, the urges that God gives us when we with hearts totally open to his will, are praying and asking him to tell us what he wants us to do and how he wants us to do it.[1]

Do I believe in my capacity to hear God?

[1] Fr. John A. Hardon (transcription of a retreat given to the Handmaids of the Precious Blood, December 1988).

That You give me the grace to accept forgiveness and to forgive others, Jesus, I trust in You.

Forgiveness is one of the most powerful forces in the world. More than the grandeur of mighty mountains, the resplendence of the starry firmament, or the compelling intricacies of the human mind, forgiveness manifests the existence of a loving God.

That's a big claim for something we all have access to and often choose to live without. For many of us forgiveness may seem attractive as an ideal but, in the reality of our lives, unattainable or undesirable. When we've been hurt, the experience feels like something has been taken away from us. And in the wake of this lack, forgiveness seems like an audacious beggar, asking us to give something costly precisely from this deficit. How is it possible? In this deprivation we only sense anger, fear, and pain. We feel that we will be consenting to live with this debt by forgiving the other. Yet, the instinct to protect ourselves and avenge the wrong are only on the surface of what is going on. Digging deeper—which is not intuitive in a place of pain—reveals something more.

Beyond the injury, there is a desire for wholeness, for restitution—what God calls "redemption." This is the reason Jesus came, to set things right by winning for us the love that restores us in full. Without trust in Jesus' redeeming love, we will try on our own for decades to fill the void, unsuccessfully. Resentment, bitterness, revenge, anger, and pride pretend to be our allies but betray us further.

Trust has the courage to shift my focus from myself and the justifications I've gathered and tended so meticulously to look at Jesus. Nothing is lost in His gaze. The heartache, the injustice, whatever the losses are, He sees completely and has the power to transform them. And we do not have to go far to find Him. Hidden in this desire for redemption is Jesus Himself, reminding us that that which is most precious within us cannot be taken: my connection to God, for "at every time and in every place, God draws close to man" (CCC 1).

Forgiveness is not sheer willpower, mere words, or a feeling. It is a *choice of the heart* to release a person from the debt they owe you, even if reconciliation with that person is not possible because of safety reasons or death. This is difficult because the one who has hurt me has broken my trust in some way. Yet, if I truly desire healing, I can't interiorly walk away; healing needs to come about precisely in the place where the wound was inflicted. The trust that was broken in relationships will only be healed by beginning to trust again within relationships. First and foremost we learn to trust God, and in this relationship of trust, I learn to receive forgiveness, this freely given love of God for us. Then in turn I am able to forgive others. It is grace that heals. If we look at the root of the word "forgive," we find *perdonare*, which in Latin signifies "to give wholeheartedly, to remit."[1]

---

[1] *English-Word Information*, s.v. "pardon," accessed April 24, 2021,

In this light we see the invitation to forgiveness as it truly is: allowing God's love to redeem the world through us. I discover that in this place of lack, I do have something to give. Something that otherwise would never have emerged, bringing out the best in me and participating in the saving mission of Jesus.

This is what the Servant of God Elisabeth Leseur lived. She never pushed her faith on her husband, Felix, but strove to love him faithfully, silently praying for his conversion. Day after day she forgave his degrading comments to her about her spiritual convictions and never let resentment build against him for the ways he tried to demoralize her. For Elisabeth it was not easy to live this steady, surrendered mercy. Looking to God, she journaled her love intermixed with anguish, knowing she could face her own heart because she had first encountered Jesus' unwavering mercy toward her. And thus Jesus could live that same unconditional love through her.

It was only after her death at a young age that her husband read her journal and found out about her immense prayer life and how earnestly she desired him to know the Lord. Felix experienced the power of Elisabeth's trust, that she knew God alone would move his heart, so present through her merciful love. Felix converted and became a Dominican priest for the remaining decades of his life. Reflecting upon his life, he shared, "Elisabeth acted upon me without my perceiving it. . . . I could never weary of admiring her moral force in the midst of a real martyrdom."[2]

https://wordinfo.info/results/pardons.

[2] Elisabeth Leseur, *Elisabeth Leseur: Selected Writings*, trans. and ed. Janet K. Ruffing (New York: Paulist Press, 2005), xxxix.

What about those of us who feel more like Felix than Elisabeth and struggle to accept forgiveness, knowing we were the guilty one? How often in my community's Hope and Healing ministry do we hear those suffering after abortion say, "I know God can forgive me, but I cannot forgive myself." Why is this? Oftentimes when we've hurt another, we begin to disdain that person simply because they represent to us our shortcomings (see, for example, 2 Sam 13:15). But if I am my own reminder of the offense, I can disdain myself. We must be careful to not place ourselves above God, thinking that what He offers is not sufficient. Here, trust allows Jesus to be the threshold of mercy, most tangibly in Confession: what He forgives *is* forgiven.

JESUS, I TRUST IN YOU

Crucified on either side of Jesus were men punished for their crimes. In anger, one of them cried out to Jesus that He should save them, if He really was the Christ (Luke 23:39). This man neither believed nor hoped in Jesus but only saw Him as a place to vent blame. The second criminal defends Jesus, saying He is innocent and asking Jesus to "remember me when you come into your kingdom" (v. 42, NRSVCE). Jesus' response to him is stunning: "Truly, I say to you, today you will be with me in Paradise" (v. 43).

What gave this "good thief" the conviction to trust Jesus in this dire moment? One wonders if this thief, who was guilty of the sentence he received, was filled with bitterness over his life shortly before his crucifixion. And upon hearing Jesus' words—"Father, forgive them; for they know not what they do" (Luke 23:34)—an unexpected sweetness swept over his heart. Here in this stockpile of misery, love was present. Not just any love, but a redeeming love, able to forgive. In Jesus the good thief recognized the one thing that was perfectly suited to restore all that was ravaged within him. It was anything but weakness to make a claim on it!

Thief that he was, this man was fully aware that he did not deserve heaven; yet he proclaimed the crucified and dying Jesus as Lord. Jesus could not wait another day to reward the faith of this man. The wealth of His goodness, once discovered, could not be contained. Nor can it be when we receive it; we must share it freely.

Jesus is very clear in His desire for us to forgive. When Peter suggests the generosity of forgiving someone seven times, Jesus says in response, "I do not say to you seven times, but seventy times seven" (Matt 18:22). He knows we do not have the strength to live the love of forgiveness, but He continues to give what we need, from His own place of lack—the Cross. This was the greatest place of deprivation for Jesus. And here He gives, gives, and gives. Straining for every breath, one might not think He had much left to give. Yet He gave His will, His tunic, His mother, His surrender, His forgiveness, His blessing, His words, His spirit, His breath, and His life. Furthermore, the Lord is truly joyful in forgiving us and in helping us to forgive, as His love is a gift that He longs for us to receive and share (Luke 15:10).

INVITATION

- Interior pain tells us something. If I have unforgiveness in my heart, I risk letting the pain I've experienced shape how I see myself. Or I can live my life wanting others to suffer simply because I am suffering. When I experience the pain of an injury, do I stop and ask the Lord what it is revealing? Is there someone I need to forgive or ask forgiveness from?

- I stumbled upon a forgiveness prayer, and the first time I saw it, it brought tears to my eyes. Over the years I had forgiven an injury and brought my heartache to the Lord in Confession, yet something was still left lingering, unresolved. This prayer powerfully acknowledges that there is a debt and that the person who owes it *cannot* pay it. It says, "I release [this person] from his debt to me and I give that debt to you Jesus. I ask you to give [this person] a blessing instead."[3] And as I would encounter any resentment, pain, or bitterness, I would repeat this prayer. It began to shift my heart and free it. This prayer becomes especially powerful when I am the cause of my own pain. *I ask You, Lord, to release me from this debt, and I give that debt to You, Jesus. I ask You to give me a blessing instead.* How do I need to implement this prayer to further receive God's mercy?

---

[3] Fr. Carlos Martins, "How to Forgive," *Pilgrimage of Mercy*, accessed March 7, 2021, https://mariagoretti.com/how-to-forgive/.

- True forgiveness can be very hard because we must relinquish our sense of power in relationships. This power can mean waiting for an apology, which may never come. It can also mean needing to be acknowledged as the one who was right, or forever holding it over their head that they hurt you. God alone can set things right. Give Him the power to heal your heart by letting go of all this, acknowledging that each of us deserves to be treated with love; but to demand love from another will never satisfy you. What am I holding on to? Is there anything blocking me in my path toward truly forgiving another?

DAY 25

That You give me all the strength I need for what is asked, Jesus, I trust in You.

Many of us know someone who never thought they would be able to finish the 26.2 miles of a marathon, but in fact did. And as every distance runner will tell you, it entails a strength beyond the physical.

When we lack energy or motivation in our lives, we can easily doubt that we will have the strength to be faithful to what God asks. We can feel like we've signed up for a marathon without the necessary training, thinking, "I don't have the strength for this task," "this conversation," or "this commitment"; yet God always provides the vigor we need to live what He is calling us to: love. Thankfully the ability to love is not simply the result of practice coupled with positive self-talk; it is a gift from God, of which we are never the source. St. Paul writes that "God chose what is weak in the world to shame the strong" (1 Cor 1:27), reminding us that our own strength cannot be the marker of our confidence.

We expect to feel a sturdiness in our capacities as we live our call to love, both with God and neighbor, as though we can coast on cruise control. Although good choices become easier to choose the more we choose them, as the journey of love progresses, we become more aware of our need for God. Far from being scary or bad, this frees us to receive the strength of His love to continue climbing the heights.

In Uganda in the mid-1880s, King Mwanga came to power. He was unfamiliar with the Christian faith that had recently been introduced to the area by missionaries and thought that their influence could be a threat to his kingdom. There were many young male pages at the court of King Mwanga, when the chief page, Charles Lwanga, was baptized and inspired some of those in his charge to learn about his new faith. Valuing the authority entrusted to him, Charles protected those he instructed against the sinful desires of the king, all the while working diligently for Mwanga's household.

Several months after Charles' baptism, King Mwanga became infuriated one day, noticing that those who had converted were not afraid to resist his sinful advances. Gathering all the pages, he demanded that all who prayed identify themselves. As much as they esteemed their lives, Charles and fourteen others stepped forward, fully aware that their obedience to the King of Heaven may cost them everything. As young as thirteen years old, and all recent converts, they sang on the way to their deaths.

What is this strength that gives courage in the face of death, that gave St. Charles Lwanga a fire of love for those who were persecuting him that was stronger than the flames that consumed his body? Surely those young men embody our belief as Christians: "I can do all things in him who strengthens me" (Phil 4:13). When we find ourselves in the midst of what will be a costly surrender if we follow God—whether that be as dramatic as witnessing our belief in Jesus at the price of our blood, or losing our friends or reputation for His sake— it may seem like God is asking the impossible. What about facing a terminal illness or that of a loved one, or even the natural decline of old age? In each of these, God is asking that we trust Him as the Lord of Life, as the Lord of the entirety of our lives. Our life, as well as our death, is in His hands. Situations that bring us to our knees, helpless, press us to seek what true strength is. Is not love at its strongest when, in our moments of deepest need, we allow His life to course through us? Do I trust that God knows how best to make my love emerge and reach out to the world? We too can experience "it is no longer I who live, but Christ who lives in me" (Gal 2:20). Trust knows we are as strong as His love.

JESUS, I TRUST IN YOU

Wrestling with a difficulty in his own spiritual journey, St. Paul pleads to be delivered from it. Instead the Lord assured him, "My grace is sufficient for thee: for my strength is made perfect in weakness" (2 Cor 12:9, KJV). Maybe God's power does not seem attractive to us. King Mwanga is only one example among many of how power is something that has been misused and abused. This may make us hesitant to welcome God's power, especially when we experience our weakness. We can only understand God's power rightly if we see it as it is, as the power of a *humble* love.

Jesus arose to meet Judas when he came to betray Him, greeting him as "[f]riend" (Matt 26:50). It was a painful moment for Jesus but tremendously sacred in His eyes. He loved Judas, so much so that in beckoning him as His apostle, Jesus wanted Judas to intimately share in His eternal glory. This rejection was further agonizing as it was cloaked in "compassion"—with a kiss.

When Judas announces that he is seeking Jesus of Nazareth, Jesus responds, "I am he" (John 18:5). At this, everyone "drew back and fell to the ground" (v.6). The power of this name instantly propelled them to the dust. Jesus was announcing that He is Almighty God, using the same words that were given to Moses when asking who the mysterious voice was in the burning bush: "I AM WHO I AM" (Exod 3:14). As they regained themselves, Jesus stood before Judas and his band as the eternal, unchanging Source without a source, with no power struggle. Not even Peter could understand this, drawing his sword in defense. But Jesus was laying down what seemed like strength to the world to wield a power far greater.

For years Judas may have been thinking that alongside Jesus he would be a part of a great earthly kingdom. As Jesus revealed that He was neither attracted to nor threatened by temporal influence, but instead held love as what triumphs over all, Judas may have disdained this plan and resented Jesus. Power and strength, in Judas' eyes, were not synonymous with love.

The sacredness of this moment was that Jesus stepped into this inner place of vulnerability that Judas refused. Here, Jesus chose to love rather than to dominate with worldly power. Jesus knew this betrayal was not taking away His dignity but was inviting it to be manifested all the more brilliantly. He was loving in a place of utter rejection; regardless of whether that love was received, Jesus would use all the power in His strength to win Judas' heart. What seemed like defeat within Judas (Matt 27:4–5) ultimately ushered in eternal salvation for all who desired it. Truly His power is made perfect in weakness.

INVITATION

- To be strong is to finally let go and let God's strength carry us. Feeling spiritually strong can be a dangerous thing, as we can think we no longer need God. However, only God will provide the strength I need. So in my daily life, can I reach out to God in my moments of need? "Lord, take care of this meeting I have today," or, "Give me patience to endure this difficult person in my life," or, "Help me persevere in this suffering." If we live like this, our daily lives will become a series of little miracles. Then Christ is truly living and loving within me. Where is God inviting me to receive His strength?

- A supernatural strength is always available to us, that we may become strong in His love. For, after Christ assures St. Paul that His power is made perfect in weakness, St. Paul finishes his thoughts by saying, "For the sake of Christ, then, I am content with weaknesses, insults, hardships, persecutions, and calamities; for when I am weak, then

I am strong" (2 Cor 12:10). A sense of misguided compassion can cause us to miss the grace God is offering us in our experience of vulnerability to *live* weakness, trusting the Lord's strength in it. For example, am I willing to accept when and how God will call me and my loved ones home to Himself in the hour of death?

• Maybe I feel as though I do not have the strength to do everything because I am trying to do more than what God is asking of me. He may be asking me to simplify my schedule, ensuring time for what is truly essential: prayer, loved ones, and the duties entrusted to me. Have I become a victim of the heresy of busyness?

That my life is a gift, Jesus, I trust in You.

When something is imposed on us, it often does not feel like a gift, even if it is wonderful. Going to church every Sunday, learning to read, or the shape of my face— the fact that it was imposed means we did not get to choose it, and until it is personally chosen, it can retain a negative quality. When we choose something, it validates it as some type of good for us. We use our wills, which is the power of our souls to decide, to consent to it as a good. In fact, we can actually choose what is bad for us because we see some apparent "good" in it. For example, we may choose to see a bad movie, knowing that it will have some vulgar qualities yet thinking it will entertain me. And for this good of entertainment, I have consented to immoral language and images. So in our freedom of will, we can choose or desire objectively bad things.

For God, it is different. Everything God wills *is* good. In creating us, God willed us, and therefore we are good. He created us because He wanted to share His goodness with us. True goodness has a contagious quality that is better articulated through the language of "sharing of itself": "Goodness is fundamentally communicative; the higher its level the more abundantly and intimately it gives itself. Whereas the friendship of a superficial soul remains totally external and a matter of the affections, the friendship of a noble soul is the generous gift of its innermost self."[1] The deeper the goodness, the more intimately it gives itself.

Now, where we can have difficulty is that we did not get to choose who we are or even *that* we are. God did. And He affirms our value, by choosing us when He has no need for us. No matter how messy our life is, He invites us to see it as He does, to consent to receive our life as the gift it is.

The more we receive this truth of our God-given goodness, the more we likewise become a vessel of that goodness to others. We want to communicate that goodness through the gift of our lives.

One powerful example of this trust was Chiara Luce Badano. Chiara was a typical teenager who assumed she was at the beginning of her life, enjoying friends, sports, and music. At seventeen, while playing tennis, she staggered off the court in pain. Soon after, she was diagnosed with aggressive bone cancer. For the next two years of her life, she battled the illness using every medical approach available. She leaned on her faith in a much more personal way, hoping that her health would be restored. However, it became clearer that the treatments were not effective, and finally, when the last method failed, Chiara found out that she was dying.

When Chiara came home from that appointment, her mom asked her if she wanted to talk. But Chiara

---

[1] Réginald Garrigou-Lagrange, *Our Savior and His Love for Us: Catholic Doctrine on the Interior Life of Christ as It Relates to Our Own Interior Life* (Gastonia, NC: TAN Books, 1999), 80–81.

refused, at least for the moment. Instead, saddened and serious, she went into her room. Twenty-five minutes later, Chiara emerged, with a light and a joy radiating out from her eyes. She had given her "yes" to God, and it had transformed her. She did not know why God was asking this of her, but she did know that He was asking it. "If you want it, then I want it too" became her motto.[2] Countless hearts were touched by Chiara in the time of her final sickness, as she was a bearer of His light, encouraging and inspiring others to trust His love with her beaming smile and words. It was almost as if Chiara was being asked the simple question, which we all encounter at some point in our lives, "Is my life being taken from me, or will I give it?"

Although it seemed she had a beautiful life prior to this, it was not until she was invited to give her life away to God and others through this suffering that it became truly luminous. If God desired her love in this way, then she would give it; Chiara knew her life was a gift. She was a radiance of the truth that can be applied to each of us: "Man ... cannot fully find himself except through a sincere gift of himself."[3] This invitation remains for each of us in everyday situations as well as in the larger scope of life. "Is my afternoon being taken from me, or will I give it as a gift?"—or my future, my plans, my health. Trust frees the heart to live the gift of my life.

---

[2] Michele Zanzucchi, *Chiara Luce: A Life Lived to the Full* (London: New City, 2007), 37, 49.

[3] Pope Paul VI, Pastoral Constitution on the Church in the Modern World *Gaudium et Spes* (December 7, 1965), §24.

JESUS, I TRUST IN YOU

At the Last Supper, Jesus plainly spoke to the apostles about His love and tried to prepare them for what lay ahead. "Father, they are your gift to me" (John 17:24, NABRE). Why did Jesus say this out loud, as it was a prayer between Him and the Father? Jesus wants us to hear His prayer to the Father, to show that we have already found a home in Them—*they are Your gift to Me*. And in that same breath, Jesus requests that they "may be with me where I am" (v. 24). It's not only that the Father gives us to the Son, but it is also that the Son deeply desires us and wants to receive us. We are not an imposition that is tolerated; we are a gift that is received and chosen.

Many who were looked down upon in Jesus' time were noticed and sought after by Jesus. Zacchaeus, a tax collector who had extorted money from the people for his own gain, was curious about who Jesus was. Being unable to see Jesus in a crowd because of his shorter height, Zacchaeus climbed a tree. As Jesus passed by, He saw the treasure of this man's life when possibly no one else did, treating him with reverence. The simple truth that Jesus desired Zacchaeus' love, even though he was living counter to the Gospel, revealed to everyone and especially Zacchaeus that his life was a gift in itself. Jesus said, "Zacchaeus, make haste and come down; for I must stay at your house today" (Luke 19:5). This man, who had gone through life unable to measure up, received Jesus with joy and, in an overspill of repentance and gratitude, gave back not double but fourfold to those he had mistreated!

Jesus wants each of us to believe Him when He calls after us, reminding us by His genuine love that we are a gift. He is no superficial friend; He shares His innermost self with us by inviting us into His relationship with the Father. He gives Himself to us as a gift as well. We can look to the Father and boldly say of Jesus, "Father, He is your gift to me, and I ask that where He is I too may be."

INVITATION

- None of us is a mistake. We have been awaited by God from all eternity. To help me see what He treasures in me, I can ask God to give me a heart full of gratitude so that I can base the choosing of my life off the truth of His vision. Is there something about my life that feels imposed? In these places, can I share my innermost self with Him and ask for the grace to choose my life by giving a definitive "yes" to the gift of my life? Accusation and desolation are the devil's tactics to make us think that we are not a gift. We need to reject these thoughts—"I am not good" or "I'm a mistake." They not only wound us but also offend God. When these thoughts arise, can I renounce them by praying, "In Your Name, Lord Jesus, I renounce the lie that . . . "

- When we feel deprived of something, it seems as though we are being robbed of something that is due to me. Are there places where I feel like my life is being taken from me? Can I look at those same areas as an opportunity to give the gift of my love? This is likely the place Jesus is most desirous of your love, believing in your capacity to give the gift of yourself.

• Our love goes a long way and helps others recognize their inherent goodness. Pray for someone who has caused you pain, that they may come to know the gift they are and live in accord with their dignity.

Day 27

That You will teach me to trust
You, Jesus, I trust in You.

At the end of a retreat, I sensed an inspiration to paint a picture of Jesus. Although I typically avoid painting faces, and using watercolor—which are both difficult for me—I began. Looking at one of my favorite renditions of Jesus, I started my painting with the most difficult part: the eyes. Without thinking much, but full of the confidence that He blesses my meager efforts, I swirled my paintbrush briefly over the two spots I designated. Seconds later I stood back in shock. They looked real. I wondered at that moment if I had really painted them! Then the nose, beard, crown of thorns, hair. It was as though someone were guiding my hand. After twenty minutes, I looked at my completed work and then glanced back to the holy card next to it, only to fall in love with the newly crafted image!

It was my hands that indeed painted it, yet I knew in the depths of my heart that it was given to me by Jesus. More than the picture itself, the experience of receiving it touched me. It seemed as though Jesus wanted me to marvel anew at the blending of our lives, and in the freedom of knowing that no shortcoming of mine limited this relationship, as long as my heart remained open to Him. Knowing that I could never have done this

on my own brought about a greater love and gratitude.

And this is the message of trust He has been teaching me all along.

Since I am the youngest of eight and a twin, the palette of my life was filled with faith and family. There was plenty of laughter, debates, and competitive games, but all of us knew what was most important in life: God.

Yet in His goodness, God did not want me to merely slide into my faith like a hand-me-down sweater. He offered a more tailored invitation to intimacy with Him. Even though I knew I was loved by generous parents whose hearts and souls were committed to bringing their children to heaven, I still experienced suffering that pierced my heart and led me to make conclusions that only compounded the pain.

I don't remember blaming God, but the injury was aggravated by not facing Him or the deep places of my heart. Without realizing it, I doubted that the Master Artist was bringing something beautiful out of my life. In every aspect of my life, I lacked courage: I did not try to excel in sports or academics and undershot in all the jobs I applied for. I hated attention. The frustration of my helplessness fueled not only the decision to be halfhearted in everything but also led to discouragement over the ways I was trying to cope, which were not working—denial, self-reliance, and avoidance.

Even though there were many good things in my life, my heart was heavy. In moments when the ache surfaced, I began to open the diary of St. Faustina, for whom I was named at my birth. Jesus would appear to her, unabashedly desiring her love and thirsting for others to know His merciful heart. St. Faustina seemed frail to me, due to her health and sensitivities, yet Jesus always saw a capacity for greatness in her love, which surprised me. Jesus was teaching St. Faustina to speak simply and openly with Him, to not be afraid.[1] This effusion of Jesus' heart, so often recorded, began to awaken my desire to be seen and known. It was only through this vulnerability of His that I could see that my own fragile heart, in its entirety, was worth unlocking.

In opening my heart, I found that Jesus was not annoyed, repelled, or deterred by anything I shared. He was tender in receiving me in my pain, and strong when pulling me out of self-pity. He was patient when I was

---

[1] Kowalska, *Diary of St. Faustina*, para. 797.

hesitant, and forthcoming when I was presumptuous. Whatever happened, I began to see He had only one goal: drawing me closer to Himself. I was learning to bring Him everything, and to have the courage to listen.

As I write this, I can see so clearly that God is redeeming *everything* in my life. He sees all the details of my thoughts and experiences and, through them, has taught me so much about the landscape of trust. I truly believe "that in everything God works for good with those who love him" (Rom 8:28). Those He placed in my life, with all their strengths and weaknesses, have ultimately focused my gaze on Him. I've learned they are not God, nor can I expect them to be, yet He resides mysteriously in each of them, longing to love me or be loved by me.

When we live in trust, nothing can hold us back from God's perfect plan of holiness for our lives. We are not perfect nor are the situations we face, but He is. As the psalmist says, "This God—his way is perfect" (Ps 18:30). The genius of His love always meets each splatter of sin and suffering with fresh strokes of His grace, transforming them into a life-giving waterfall.

JESUS, I TRUST IN YOU

Before Jesus gave Himself totally on Calvary, He desired our attention. Scourged and crowned with thorns, He was brought out in front of the crowd gathered, as Pilate dramatically announced, "Behold the man!" (John 19:5, ESV). The eyes of all were fixed on Jesus. *Behold the man.* Fully God, yet fully man. Disfigured by the lashes,

Jesus did not try to explain that this was not who He is, or that this was unjust.

Jesus stood motionless, without any escape route in mind or heart. He was thinking of us. Receiving the coldness, hatred, and disgust of the crowd, He wanted to be there for us. The external sufferings were only a window into what He embraced in that moment. In His person He was taking on the shame of all sin, the humiliation of rejection, and all that we would be tempted to evade. But covered with every revilement, Jesus radiated a supreme dignity. Far from distancing Himself from us in the very place of our misery, His eyes speak the truth that His heart contains: *Let My love be your very own.*

When Jesus' heart was pierced on the Cross, "at once there came out blood and water" (John 19:34); it was the final gift from Him who had given everything He had. This last offering, the emptying of the contents of His heart entirely, show the disposition of Jesus toward us: *for* us and *with* us.

The blood and water that spilled from His heart was left to fall to the ground like something inconsequential, but it was exceptionally precious. That which flowed out of His heart was a stream that cleansed and brought new life for us. "O Blood and water which gushed forth from the Heart of Jesus as a fount of mercy for us, I trust in you."[2]

Jesus' heart being poured out was not an isolated event but an exposé on true life. Even until the very end, Jesus was teaching us. Revered as a "rabboni," which means teacher, He taught how to live in right relationship with God. As fully God and fully man, Jesus, in

---

[2] Kowalska, *Diary of St. Faustina*, para. 187.

His very person, is the living revelation of how to love the Father through trust—a trust that shares the *whole* heart. And that it is possible through Him.

INVITATION

- When we have failed the Lord, we can doubt that He will continue to teach us how to trust or that we will ever be able to learn. The Lord is always inviting us to a deeper trust. As we recognize the invitations to trust and live them, they continue to challenge us. When it gets hard to trust, do I assume I am doing something wrong? What makes me doubt my ability to trust?

- When we are scared to let another into the deep places of our hearts, we close the door in distrust. Shame can also hold us back from trust, believing we are the wounds we carry. Jesus does not want us to hide but invites us to let ourselves be seen. Find an image of Jesus you love and spend time looking at Jesus look at you.

- When we begin to learn to trust God, it can be hard not to want others in our life to continually speak into our decisions and direct us. While it is good to have trusted spiritual guides, God speaks to us in our hearts personally and wants us to start taking the small leaps of faith to follow Him. Am I struggling to believe that He actually trusts my capacity to follow His promptings?

That You are my Lord and my God, Jesus, I trust in You.

In the early 1920s, a newly married couple began a life together, passionate about building a better world than they had known growing up through World War I. God was not a part of their equation for peace and prosperity, as neither saw how His supposed "love" was meeting the needs of the turbulent world.

They decided to raise their one daughter, Lucette, without any acknowledgement of God. Yet, Lucette's maternal grandmother secretly arranged for her to be baptized at the local parish, concerned that her grand-daughter would be brought up bereft of faith. Finding out afterward, the couple was enraged and moved away, threatening their Christian parents that they would have no contact with them if they ever mentioned God to their daughter.[1]

God was far from being out of the picture, though. One day, outside their house in Morocco, young Lucette looked up to see a magnificent sunset after a sandstorm. The immense beauty stunned her. She felt within it a being who created it and knew in that moment "all was

---

[1] Mother Veronica Namoyo Le Goulard, *A Memory for Wonders* (San Francisco: Ignatius Press, 1993), 23.

from him."[2] A few years later, while looking at a shopping catalog of her mother's, Lucette stumbled across a picture of a crucifix. As she looked at the man fastened to the cross, her heart recognized that it was the same being who created the sunset. She did not know the word "God" but was indeed praying to Him.[3]

In this, God broke through to reach a heart that deserved a chance to know Him. Lucette still struggled to make sense of life, trying to navigate through the thick tensions in her family, the contradictions in her parents' political views, and her own propensity for mischief. But over time, not only was God drawing her to the Catholic Church, but she subsequently felt His call to become a cloistered religious sister. To live for God alone was the complete antithesis of her parents' desires.

What seemed like the final blow to her parents' relationship with God eventually became what would open their hearts to Him. They could not comprehend that with all they had done to shut God out of Lucette's life, He had still become so central to her. As the storm of disapproval and misunderstanding subsided, all that was left was the unexplainable marvel that God's light had shone through. Lucette had indeed become the "sunset" for her parents, a proof of the existence of His love. Or more fittingly, her life had become a true image of that man fastened to a cross, whose sacrifice they didn't understand but would come to know as the deepest love. Lucette, who became Mother Veronica Namoyo, saw God's faithfulness in revealing to her family that His love was in fact meeting the needs of the world.

[2] Le Goulard, *A Memory for Wonders*, 30.
[3] Le Goulard, *A Memory for Wonders*, 41.

Who is God? More breathtaking than crimson hues in the sky, He permeates the existence of all despite the locked doors of human hearts. He is always searching for the slightest opening in our hearts to reveal Himself—He who has a height and depth that cannot be measured or contained! He manifests Himself quietly to a child—He, whose grandeur cannot be matched. Vaster than our tiny scope of understanding, He invites us to stand in awe of Him, whom we come to know and yet never fully comprehend.

Still, we can doubt that Jesus is truly God and lives up to His claims as Savior, misunderstanding Him to be an ideology, a life coach, or even a threat. Recovering addicts are often those who surprisingly have no doubts in this regard. In their toughest moments, helpless in the face of their addictions, they have come to the undeniable realization that they are but creatures. This awareness of their inability to live a life of freedom without God was the pivotal turning point of grace for them.

We're all offered these situations. Every time I encounter my limits—whether it is struggling with infertility, a disabling accident, a broken engagement, or failing licensing tests—an invitation to freedom awaits. God is the Limitless One who at this very juncture wants to be our Savior. When we turn with trust to God in these situations, they truly become the crucial place where we come to know personally that God is *my* Savior. The way He reveals Himself to each individual is tailored to the doubts of each one of us. We don't have to go far to find God, for in the very place of our struggle, He stands and waits to be discovered.

JESUS, I TRUST IN YOU

After Jesus rose from the dead, He appeared to the disciples, but Thomas was not there. Upon hearing their report, Thomas claimed, "Unless I see in his hands the print of the nails, and place my finger in the mark of the nails, and place my hand in his side, I will not believe" (John 20:25). Thomas knew the Resurrection of Jesus was no trivial matter and wanted to be convicted of its truth. For the Resurrection was the proof that Jesus was indeed the Son of God, conquering death and inviting all to the unending life of God.

The following week, Thomas and the apostles were gathered behind shut doors, when Jesus returned. He turned to Thomas and invited him to place his hand in His wounds and to "not be faithless, but believing" (John 20:27). As Thomas willingly complied, he exclaimed, "My Lord and my God!" (v. 28).

Looking to Jesus, we see the Creator of the heavens and the earth. And after He suffered and died for His people, and rose from the dead, He could not leave behind the one who doubted Him. Full of humility, Jesus meets Thomas where he is at. This is what Jesus did in becoming man and continually does for each one of us, knowing that this very type of love will bring *us* to where *He* is. It may have pained Jesus that Thomas put conditions on his belief in the Lord's power, but Jesus was not upset with Thomas. The pain Jesus felt was a pain of knowing that someone He loves does not know Him. Seeing His wounds, Thomas realizes he is actually encountering his own wounds, taken up by Jesus and now glorified. *My* Lord and *my* God.

Knowing countless souls would never see or touch Him in those days following Easter Sunday, the Lord made known through Thomas' doubt His desire that all should never fear to approach Him in honesty. Jesus longs to be given the opportunity to show Himself anew in the questioning heart and thus awaken a personal knowledge of His love. Promising a greater blessing for trusting without seeing, Jesus proclaimed, "Blessed are those who have not seen and yet believe" (John 20:29).

INVITATION

- Although we are finite creatures, Jesus wants us to have a boundless trust in Him, because our trust is based in one who is eternal. Jesus, through the power of His death and Resurrection, carries us beyond our limitations. Have I ever experienced the conviction in my heart that Jesus died for *me*? If I have not yet, pray for the grace to truly know Jesus as *my* Lord and *my* God.

- It is good to remember the particular ways God has revealed Himself to us. It may be connected to how He is inviting you to manifest Him to those in your life. Are we willing to be the "sunset" for others? If God has revealed Himself to you through a long, steady, patient love, is God asking me to be that for another? If I've come to know Him in my love for the Eucharist, can I share that with others?

• Baptism is the most singular grace offered to us, to receive the new life of Jesus' Resurrection. Although it is not recommended to secretly baptize another (because of its gravity), the power to bring God's presence within the soul and awaken it to truth is incomparable. Do I know the day of my baptism, the day when He truly became *my* Lord? We can renew our baptismal promises not only at Easter but every year on the anniversary of our own baptism, asking for the grace to be faithful to those promises.

That I am Your beloved one, Jesus, I trust in You.

During his travels, Gonzalo, a wealthy merchant, fell in love with a woman who was a poor weaver, Catalina. Overcoming the societal prejudices, Gonzalo married her even though this meant being disinherited by his family. Their marriage would not have been possible without this sacrifice, and it deepened their love, which profoundly impacted their youngest son. As he grew up, the young St. John of the Cross would likewise see an invitation to intimacy when the love of God captured his own heart, asking him to leave all behind and become a Carmelite friar.

As St. John of the Cross chose external poverty to be united to Christ, he saw that Christ had chosen far more than the relinquishing of material goods to be united to us. Christ became poor for our sake (2 Cor 8:9) so that we could receive His immense wealth of divine love: that of being totally chosen by Him forever. Christ chose us; Christ chose to become man so that we could eternally be His beloved ones. St. John of the Cross thus saw that the way we can receive this deepening union and wealth of God Himself is to cling in faith to Jesus, while making the gift to God of our interior wealth. This treasure is our will, our ability to choose.

Our will is tremendously valuable since the choice to love another is sacred, and God thus longs to be chosen by us. In giving God our will, we do not forfeit this wondrous gift but rather make the ultimate choice with it. When we give God our will, not only are we choosing to love Him, but we are also choosing to give Him complete control to *keep* the doors of our heart open. God thus has free and total access to my heart and can pour Himself into me so that I can receive Him fully and give my love fully.

Choosing to give ourselves in this way unites us to God deeply and is the best way to live our beloved-ness. In this gift, God's will and my will become one. The invitation to spiritual poverty, which St. John of the Cross spoke of, is a necessary component toward divine intimacy.

Spiritual poverty is a very hidden yet powerful part of every saint's story. Such a concept is completely foreign in a culture that idolizes choosing whatever *I* want, whenever *I* want, because *I* want. Even if we are trying to live a moral life, we can spend our days without God being a part of our decisions. When we fall in love, we stop making decisions just for ourselves; we are compelled to do everything out of deference to the beloved. And with God, we begin to desire what He desires so that we are not separated from Him in any way.

The giving of our will to God is usually gradual, over a lifetime. We choose to let go of our inclinations by mortifying ourselves in little ways. For example, I could hold my tongue in conversation to let others speak, forego an activity I enjoy so that I can help someone instead, or fast for a specific intention. God inspires and completes this in us. Exercising our will in this way—by surrendering our preferences for the sake of love—frees our hearts from the desires and attachments that keep us from a deeper union with Him. If I leave my will unchecked and give way to every impulse, my efforts to grow in relationship with God will be thwarted. This same type of mortification can be seen in bigger decisions as well. St. John of the Cross, instead of following his desire to spend his life in prayer and study, whole-heartedly accepted the call of God to go out preaching, offering spiritual direction, and reforming the Carmelite order. By not placing our trust in what we want, we can trust that what God ultimately chooses for us will bring us into a profound experience of oneness with Him.

When we allow the Lord to direct us, we "abandon" ourselves into the arms of the one who alone fills our hearts. No matter if we have clarity or darkness, con-solation or dryness, everything becomes a path to Him when we entrust ourselves to Him.

With our hearts totally open to receiving God, we are able to give Him His very own love in return. "This is the soul's deep satisfaction and happiness: To see that it gives God more than it is worth in itself, the very divine light and divine heat that are given to it."[1] Trust at its finest is abandoning ourselves totally to God.

JESUS, I TRUST IN YOU

The typical way a man in Jesus' time would have pro-posed to a woman was to invite her and her family to

---

[1] St. John of the Cross, *Living Flame of Love*, stanza 3, lines 79–80, in Kavanaugh and Rodriguez, ed., *The Collected Works of St. John of the Cross*, 706–707.

gather with him and his family for a meal. There would be a blessing over the wine and the man would offer the woman his chalice to drink. If she drank from it, this was a sign of her agreement and the one life they would share. He would leave that evening to go to prepare a house for them, and continue their communication through a best man, a friend of the groom. When the lodgings were ready, he would come back for her and, wedding her, bring her home to live together.[2] Knowing this, the apostles at the Last Supper had no illusions about what Jesus was saying as He handed them His chalice and spoke of preparing a place for them at His Father's house (John 14:2–3). Jesus was offering Himself to them, to live one life with them eternally.

We know God's love cannot be captured by using our relational terms, as it is beyond these and yet the source of all love. Spousal love is the closest relationship St. Paul could relate God's love to (Eph 5:21–33), because marriage is a union based on an exclusive, total, self-giving love. Through Christ, we are invited into a new type of spousal love.[3] In Him perfectly exists the union of God and man, and we are now offered the possibility to become one with God forever.

Jesus, on the night of the Last Supper, prayed to the Father, "[T]hat they may be one, even as we are one" (John 17:11), "that the love with which you have loved me may be in them, and I in them" (v.26). Jesus was turning the apostles' hearts to this source of life,

---

[2] Maurice Lamm, *The Jewish Way in Love and Marriage* (San Francisco: Harper & Row, 1980), chap. 15.

[3] Angelo Cardinal Scola, *The Nuptial Mystery* (Grand Rapids, MI: Wm. B. Eerdmans, 2005), 11.

this oneness of the Father and the Son, and to the love between them that is the Holy Spirit.

In the midst of the apostles' awe, Jesus would confirm this humbling truth: that union with Him is better than any expectation. That same night, Jesus said to the apostles, "[A]part from me you can do nothing.... Abide in my love" (John 15:5, 9). Jesus wanted the apostles—and each of us—to know that in His love they can live with trustful abandon in every circumstance. When life is seen through this lens—that God seeks each of us as His beloved, and He is our Beloved—everything changes.

INVITATION

- Jesus shows us the way to live our identity as loved and chosen by Him. It can sound soft, but it entails the courage to believe in a love we often do not see or feel in times of difficulty. Studying the life of Jesus helps us come to know how He chooses to love so that we can recognize how He desires to live His life in us. Do we have a sense of Jesus' heart, what His desires are, and how He would act in different situations?

- The world wants us to think that we are insignificant creatures that do not have immortality. No matter our state in life, God pursues us as His beloved. And His will for our lives is the best way of receiving and living that invitation. While living more simply on a material level can help create more space in our hearts for God, our willingness to give the interior wealth of our wills to God allows Him to truly live one life with us. How is God inviting me to live more simply? Can I ask for the grace to desire what He desires, that in moving my heart, I may to begin choosing Him in the continual decisions of my day?

• We may doubt our capacity to love like this—by giving our whole wills—but because God is God, His plan for us to live true to our beloved-ness is powerful. Like a dam, His grace is held back only to await our consent. Are we willing to surrender to His uniting love? Do we believe that He provides the very gift of Himself to live this call to greatness?

DAY 30

Jesus, I Trust in You:
The Blessing of Openness

Remember when the apostles were caught in a raging storm and Jesus appeared, standing on the water and saying, "Take heart, it is I; have no fear" (Matt 14:27)? On the boat, Peter looked to Jesus on the water. In that gaze, Jesus' eternal love and Peter's passing fears collided and awakened Peter's trust to live life with Jesus, wherever He was. Peter responded boldly, "Lord, if it is you, bid me *come* to you on the water" (v. 28, emphasis added). As unlikely of a request as it was, what Peter said showed that he knew the heart of Jesus.

And how many times had Peter heard it—*Come to me all who labor and are heavy burdened; Let all the little children come to Me; Come, follow Me; All who are thirsty, come to Me; Come down, Zacchaeus; My Father and I will come to you.* Jesus' quintessential message is just that— *Come.* That is the epitome of Jesus' desire—*Come.* Sure enough, through the howling winds and waves, Jesus summoned Peter: "Come" (Matt 14:29).

This was the whole reason Jesus became man, to be able to say this word to us—*Come.* Jesus, in His life, death, and Resurrection, opens the doors to eternity for us, forever affirming His openness to us. "Come, O blessed of my Father, inherit the kingdom prepared for you from the foundation of the world" (Matt 25:34).

As a culture, we have been confused, frustrated, angry, and fearful, trying to navigate the ups and downs of life without God. We don't know what is best for us. We don't know how to make ourselves happy, or what we need to find peace or be healed. We can't be our own compass, but thankfully, Jesus offers to meet us in a place where He alone *saves* us, ever leading us toward the harbor of unending life.

Where is Jesus summoning us to "Come"? Where is this tried-and-true place of encounter in our lives?

The place Jesus meets us most intimately is on the Cross. Here, in giving the total gift of Himself, we find the greatest expression of mercy, His unconditional love for us. Likewise, in Jesus on the Cross, there is no greater trust than in this sacred encounter between Him and the Father. Jesus, thinking of us while on the Cross, trusted in the Father's goodness. Jesus told St. Faustina, "The greater the misery of a soul, the greater its right to My mercy; [urge] all souls to trust in the unfathomable abyss of My mercy, because I want to save them all. On the cross, the fountain of My mercy was opened wide by the lance for all souls—no one have I excluded!"[1]

Jesus' trust won us access to His *unfathomable* mercy. Our sins and troubles are simply no match for His merciful love. He only asks us to respond to His total self-gift of mercy with one thing: our trust. Thus, *trust* must be our total self-gift back to Him, in love.

When we face situations in life that make us know that we are not God, we encounter the Cross of Christ. We may resent and reject these times that we are being asked to

---

[1] Kowalska, *Diary of St. Faustina*, para. 1182.

trust God, thinking life would be better without them. Yet if we walk away, we shut our hearts in the very place Jesus is offering His life to us. Trust draws us to choose Jesus, even when He is on the Cross, giving us the strength to surmount all difficulties to be with Him and to receive the mercy powerfully flowing from His heart to ours.

Reading these pages, maybe you've wanted to hear me say that it has been easy ever since that day when trust came alive in my own heart. *But it is not easy.* It can be tremendously difficult. Yet, finding the treasure of trust has been incredibly worthwhile, unlocking a gratitude in my heart for the one whose love transforms all things.

Trust challenges all of us, every day. We need God's grace to keep the doors of our hearts open when we'd rather shut them. Yet Jesus lived with His heart totally open in every situation. He never refused anyone His love.

He shared the beatitudes, outlining the path that allows us to live this same freedom. *Blessed are the poor in spirit, those who mourn, the meek, those who hunger and thirst for righteous' sake, the merciful, the pure in heart, the peacemakers, those who are persecuted for my sake* . . . (see Matt 5:3–12).

The invitation of the beatitudes is to live by allowing the pierced places of our hearts to be the place of encounter with Jesus and His wealth of infinite mercy. While we will suffer in this life, we will learn we can trust, because we find a love that makes us whole, whatever we've been through. We see our pierced heart as a doorway to receiving a wider share of His heart, becoming a vessel of that love for others. Living the beatitudes is in fact the flowing out of God's love through us to the world. Truly, in Him we will be forever *blessed.*

But a lot is at stake. If we do not trust God, we'll miss the love He is pouring out for us. Whatever we begin to trust now, we will receive for all eternity: death or life. The suffering of the cross passes; the life it brings is unending. We will *never* regret trusting God; in heaven we will ceaselessly praise Him for each opportunity that He gave us to trust Him.

Thinking back to that moment years ago when God inspired the Litany of Trust, I remember I had been looking at the simple crucifix in my room. And even now, He is still reaching out from the Cross, offering us what is best for our souls. No matter what our background or circumstances, the vastness of God's love always finds an opportunity to invite us to trust Him and thus share in His glory.

Trusting Jesus every day changes the course of history—it makes Him present in a world thirsty for His love. He comes to live and breathe His life in and through us, giving us the desire to love people we've never met, suffer for people who hate us, and to call every person our brother and sister. There are no limits to what God can do in our lives when we trust His mercy.

Our Blessed Mother Mary lived this and wants our hearts to be filled to overflowing. May we entrust ourselves to her maternal intercession, she whom the Father entrusted His only Son, so that we too may receive the fullness of life. For Jesus said to St. Faustina, "I desire to grant unimaginable graces to those souls who trust in My mercy."[2]

Jesus, I trust in You.

---

[2] Kowalska, *Diary of St. Faustina*, para. 687.

The Litany of Trust

From the belief that I have to earn Your love
Deliver me, Jesus.
From the fear that I am unlovable
Deliver me, Jesus.
From the false security that I have what it takes
Deliver me, Jesus.
From the fear that trusting You will leave
me more destitute
Deliver me, Jesus.
From all suspicion of Your words and promises
Deliver me, Jesus.
From the rebellion against childlike dependency
on You
Deliver me, Jesus.
From refusals and reluctances in accepting Your will
Deliver me, Jesus.
From anxiety about the future
Deliver me, Jesus.
From resentment or excessive preoccupation
with the past
Deliver me, Jesus.
From restless self-seeking in the present moment
Deliver me, Jesus.
From disbelief in Your love and presence
Deliver me, Jesus.
From the fear of being asked to give more than I have
Deliver me, Jesus.
From the belief that my life has no meaning or worth
Deliver me, Jesus.

From the fear of what love demands
Deliver me, Jesus.
From discouragement
Deliver me, Jesus.

That You are continually holding me sustaining me,
loving me
Jesus, I trust in you.
That Your love goes deeper than my sins and failings,
and transforms me
Jesus, I trust in you.
That not knowing what tomorrow brings is an
invitation to lean on You
Jesus, I trust in you.
That you are with me in my suffering
Jesus, I trust in you.
That my suffering, united to Your own, will bear fruit
in this life and the next
Jesus, I trust in you.
That You will not leave me orphan, that You are
present in Your Church
Jesus, I trust in you.
That Your plan is better than anything else
Jesus, I trust in you.
That You always hear me and in Your goodness always
respond to me
Jesus, I trust in you.
That You give me the grace to accept forgiveness and
to forgive others
Jesus, I trust in you.

That You give me all the strength I need for
what is asked
Jesus, I trust in you.
That my life is a gift
Jesus, I trust in you.
That You will teach me to trust You
Jesus, I trust in you.
That You are my Lord and my God
Jesus, I trust in you.
That I am Your beloved one
Jesus, I trust in you.

Amen.

About the Sisters of Life

Founded in 1991 by John Cardinal O'Connor, the Sisters of Life are Catholic religious women who are captivated by the truth of the beauty of every human person, created in God's image and likeness. Immersed in Eucharistic prayer within a vibrant community life, the Sisters seek to help each person experience themselves as sacred, valuable, and worthy of love.

Visit SistersOfLife.org to learn more about:

- Prayer
- Crisis Pregnancy Help
- Weekend Retreats
- Hope & Healing after Abortion
- Evangelization/Speaking Requests
- College Student Outreach
- End-of-Life Resources
- Co-Workers of Life
- Vocations Information